HOW TO PASS THE CPA EXAM:
A SYSTEM FOR SUCCESS
2015 Edition

TABLE OF CONTENTS

HOW TO PASS THE CPA EXAM

The *How to Pass the CPA Exam: A System for Success* booklet is a free guide that explains how candidates can register for, study for, and pass the CPA exam. The purpose of this booklet is to answer all of your Frequently Asked Questions and help you develop and implement a system for success for the exam, which includes

1. **Becoming familiar with the exam process, including the exam's purpose, coverage, preparation methods, format, administration, grading, and pass rates**

2. **Conceptualizing the subject matter tested**

3. **Perfecting your question-answering techniques**

4. **Planning and practicing exam execution**

5. **Developing the confidence you need to succeed!**

Each of these five steps is discussed and illustrated on the following pages. Gleim removes the "mystique" of the CPA exam by providing you with the answers, information, and tools you need to arrive at the test center with a head start **and** the confidence necessary to PASS.

"EXAM SUCCESS GUARANTEED!"

The Gleim CPA Review System GUARANTEES that you will pass each section on the first try. Visit www.gleim.com/CPAguarantees to learn more about our guarantees. Because we identify and focus on your weak areas, you will not spend any more time preparing than is necessary to guarantee success.

ii

Gleim Publications, Inc.
P.O. Box 12848
University Station
Gainesville, Florida 32604
(888) 87-GLEIM or (888) 874-5346
(352) 375-0772
Fax: (352) 375-6940
Internet: www.gleim.com
Email: admin@gleim.com

For updates to this 2015 printing of *How to Pass the CPA Exam: A System for Success*

Go To: www.gleim.com/CPAupdate

Or: Email update@gleim.com with **CPA SFS 2015** in the subject line. You will receive our current update as a reply.

Updates are available until the next edition is published.

ISBN: 978-1-58194-547-8 *CPA Review: Auditing*
ISBN: 978-1-58194-552-2 *CPA Review: Business*
ISBN: 978-1-58194-553-9 *CPA Review: Financial*
ISBN: 978-1-58194-554-6 *CPA Review: Regulation*
ISBN: 978-1-58194-560-7 *How to Pass the CPA Exam: A System for Success*

Returns of books purchased from bookstores and other resellers should be made to the respective bookstore or reseller. For more information regarding the Gleim Return Policy, please contact our offices at (800) 874-5346 or visit www.gleim.com/returnpolicy.

Environmental Statement -- This book is printed on high-quality, environmentally friendly groundwood paper, sourced from certified sustainable forests and produced either TCF (totally chlorine-free) or ECF (elementally chlorine-free). Our recyclable paper is more porous than coated paper, so we recommend marking it with a non-bleed-through highlighter.

This publication is designed to provide accurate and authoritative information with regard to the subject matter covered. It is sold with the understanding that the publisher is not engaged in rendering legal, accounting, or other professional service.

If legal advice or other expert assistance is required, the services of a competent professional person should be sought.

(From a declaration of principles jointly adopted by a Committee of the American Bar Association and a Committee of Publishers.)

REVIEWERS AND CONTRIBUTORS

Garrett W. Gleim, B.S., CPA (not in public practice), received a Bachelor of Science degree from The Wharton School at the University of Pennsylvania. Mr. Gleim coordinated the production staff, reviewed the manuscript, and provided production assistance throughout the project.

Grady M. Irwin, J.D., is a graduate of the University of Florida College of Law, and he has taught in the University of Florida College of Business. Mr. Irwin provided substantial editorial assistance throughout the project.

Michael Kustanovich, M.A., CPA, is a graduate of Ben-Gurion University of the Negev in Israel. He is a Lecturer of Accountancy in the Department of Accountancy at the University of Illinois at Urbana-Champaign. He has worked in the audit departments of KPMG and PWC and as a financial accounting lecturer in the Department of Economics of Ben-Gurion University of the Negev. Mr. Kustanovich provided substantial editorial assistance throughout the project.

D. Scott Lawton, B.S., is a graduate of Brigham Young University-Idaho and Utah Valley University. He has worked as an auditor for the Utah State Tax Commission. Mr. Lawton provided substantial editorial assistance throughout the project.

Lawrence Lipp, J.D., CPA (Registered), is a graduate from the Levin College of Law and the Fisher School of Accounting at the University of Florida. Mr. Lipp provided substantial editorial assistance throughout the project.

Jerry D. Mathis, CPA, graduated from the Fisher School of Accounting at the University of Florida. He has public accounting experience in the areas of tax compliance, tax controversy, and transaction consulting. Mr. Mathis provided substantial editorial assistance throughout the project.

A PERSONAL THANKS

This manual would not have been possible without the extraordinary effort and dedication of Jacob Brunny, Julie Cutlip, Eileen Nickl, Jake Pettifor, Teresa Soard, Justin Stephenson, Joanne Strong, Elmer Tucker, and Candace Van Doren, who typed the entire manuscript and all revisions and drafted and laid out the diagrams and illustrations in this book.

The authors also appreciate the production and editorial assistance of Jessica Felkins, James Harvin, Kristen Hennen, Jeanette Kerstein, Katie Larson, Diana León, Cary Marcous, Shane Rapp, Drew Sheppard, and Martha Willis.

The authors also appreciate the critical reading assistance of Jared Armenti, Coryn Brewer, Ellen Buhl, Paul Davis, Jack Hahne, Bethany Harris, Nathan Kaplan, Melissa Leonard, Yating Li, Monica Metz, Tyler Rankin, Daniel Sinclair, Tingwei Su, Nanan Toure, Diana Weng, and Kenneth Wilbur.

Finally, we appreciate the encouragement, support, and tolerance of our families throughout this project.

STUDY UNIT ONE
THE CPA EXAMINATION: AN OVERVIEW
AND PREPARATION INTRODUCTION

(8 pages of outline)

CBT-e Exam

Gleim Section Title	Auditing	Business	Financial	Regulation
AICPA Formal Title	Auditing & Attestation	Business Environment & Concepts	Financial Accounting & Reporting	Regulation
Acronym	AUD	BEC	FAR	REG
Exam Length	4 hours	3 hours	4 hours	3 hours
Testlets:				
Multiple-Choice	3, 30 questions each	3, 24 questions each	3, 30 questions each	3, 24 questions each
Task-Based Simulations	1 with 7 TBS	0	1 with 7 TBS	1 with 6 TBS
Written Communications	0	3	0	0

This study unit will give you an overview of the CPA exam and outline our suggested method of preparation.

1.1 FOLLOW THESE STEPS TO PASS THE EXAM

1. Scan this Gleim *How to Pass the CPA Exam: A System for Success* booklet and note where to revisit later in your studying process to obtain a deeper understanding of the CPA exam and how to prepare for it.

    a. *How to Pass the CPA Exam: A System for Success* has seven study units:

        Study Unit 1: The CPA Examination: An Overview and Preparation Introduction
        Study Unit 2: AICPA Content Specification Outlines and Skill Specification Outlines
        Study Unit 3: Content Preparation, Test Administration, and Performance Grading
        Study Unit 4: Multiple-Choice Questions
        Study Unit 5: Task-Based Simulations and Written Communications
        Study Unit 6: Preparing to Pass the CPA Exam
        Study Unit 7: How to Take the CPA Exam

    b. Additionally, the AICPA requires that all candidates review the tutorial and sample tests at www.aicpa.org.

2. BEFORE you begin studying, you may wish to take a **Diagnostic Quiz** at www.gleim.com/QuizCPA or use our Gleim Diagnostic Quiz App for iPhone, iPod Touch, and Android.

    a. The Diagnostic Quiz includes a representative sample of 40 multiple-choice questions and can help determine which section of the exam you want to take first and/or how much time you need to devote to studying particular topic areas.

    b. When you are finished, you can access a Review Session and consult with a **Personal Counselor** to better focus your review on any areas in which you have less confidence.

3. Follow the steps outlined in Study Unit 6, Subunit 7, "How to Use the Gleim Review System." This is the **study plan** that our most successful candidates adhere to. Study until you have reached your **desired proficiency level** (e.g., 75%) for each study unit.

    a. As you proceed, be sure to check any **Updates** that may have been released.

        1) All online components will be updated automatically.
        2) Updates for the printed book can be viewed at www.gleim.com/CPAupdate, or you can have them emailed to you. See the information box in the top right corner of page ii for details.

    b. **Review this *How to Pass the CPA Exam: A System for Success* booklet** and become completely comfortable with what will be expected from you on test day.

4. Shortly before your test date, take an **Exam Rehearsal** (complimentary with the CPA Review System) at www.gleim.com/RehearseCPA.

    a. The Gleim Exam Rehearsal is designed to emulate the CPA test-taking experience at Prometric.

    b. This timed and scored exam tests you not only on the content you have studied, but also on the question-answering and time-management techniques you have learned throughout the Gleim study process.

    c. When you have completed the exam, consult with your Personal Counselor to discuss where you should **focus your review during the final days before your exam** (question-answering techniques, time management, specific content areas, etc.).

5. **Take and PASS** your selected section of the CPA exam!

    a. When you have completed the exam, please contact Gleim at www.gleim.com/feedbackCPA with your **suggestions, comments, and corrections**. We want to know how well we prepared you for your testing experience.

1.2 PURPOSE OF THE EXAM

The CPA examination is designed to measure professional competence in auditing, business law, taxation, accounting, and related business topics, including

1.   The command of adequate technical knowledge
2.   The ability to apply such knowledge skillfully and with good judgment
3.   An understanding of professional responsibilities

Passing this exam validates and confirms your professional accounting education and requires your complete dedication and determination. The benefits include higher salary, increased confidence and competence, and recognition as a member of an elite group of professionals.

1.3 AMERICAN INSTITUTE OF CERTIFIED PUBLIC ACCOUNTANTS (AICPA)

The AICPA is the national professional organization of CPAs in particular and professional accountants in general. The AICPA determines/prepares the content and scoring of the Uniform Certified Public Accountant Examination. Study Unit 3, Subunit 3, contains more information.

Obtain AICPA Student Affiliate membership for FREE! College graduates who have not yet passed the CPA exam may obtain a discounted CPA Candidate membership for $50. Information regarding all memberships can be obtained from the AICPA website at www.aicpa.org.

1.4 NATIONAL ASSOCIATION OF STATE BOARDS OF ACCOUNTANCY (NASBA)

NASBA's mission is to enhance the effectiveness of state boards of accountancy in meeting their regulatory responsibilities. It is also a major component of the computerized CPA exam. As part of the exam application process, NASBA issues a Notice To Schedule (NTS) to each CPA candidate after completion of an application. While applications may be made and forwarded to individual State Boards, NASBA handles some, or all, of the application process for most State Boards. NASBA also receives all CPA scores from the AICPA and records them in their National Candidate Database before forwarding the grades to individual State Boards, which ultimately send the grades to individual CPA candidates.

1.5 STATE BOARDS OF ACCOUNTANCY

All 50 states (and the District of Columbia, Commonwealth of the Northern Mariana Islands, Guam, Puerto Rico, and the Virgin Islands) have an administrative agency that administers the laws and rules that regulate the practice of public accounting. Each of these 55 jurisdictions contracts with the AICPA to use the AICPA's Uniform CPA Examination.

The rules and procedures for applying to take the exam and becoming licensed to practice public accounting vary by jurisdiction. Accordingly, you should contact your state board for a CPA exam application form. With the form, you will receive that board's rules, regulations, and directions to you as a CPA candidate.

Visit our website at www.gleim.com/stateboards to access up-to-date State Board CPA requirements. You can find the state boards' contact information at www.nasba.org.

1.6 CPA EXAM FOR INTERNATIONAL CANDIDATES

August of 2011 was the inaugural offering of the Uniform CPA Examination outside the U.S. The international exam is offered only in English, has the same licensure requirements, and is the same as the current U.S. exam. The international exam is administered during the same testing windows as for domestic test-takers (i.e., Jan/Feb, April/May, July/Aug, and Oct/Nov), and international exam scores will be released on the same timeline as domestic scores. In addition to passing the exam, international candidates must meet educational and experience requirements.

International testing is available in Brazil, Japan, Bahrain, Kuwait, Lebanon, and the UAE. A candidate's residency status determines his or her testing center eligibility. For example, a citizen or permanent resident of Argentina may take the exam in either the U.S. or Brazil. To see where they can sit for the exam, candidates should consult the International Testing Center Eligibility Table at www.nasba.org/exams/internationalexam/.

The jurisdictions through which candidates can apply to take the CPA exam in an international location can also be found at the NASBA website listed above. Prospective candidates must select the U.S. jurisdiction (i.e., a state board of accountancy) to which they will apply, contact the board of accountancy in that jurisdiction to obtain application materials, and submit the completed applications and required fees as instructed. After receiving the NTS, candidates may then register to take the examination in an international location through the NASBA website.

1.7 SUBJECT MATTER -- AICPA AND GLEIM

The AICPA publishes Content Specification Outlines (CSOs), which outline the subject matter tested on the CPA exam. The CSOs have three levels: areas, groups, and topics.

I. Area
    A. Group
        1. Topic

The CSOs for each of the four sections of the CPA exam are presented verbatim in Study Unit 2, which begins on page 9. We have also provided cross-references to the study units and subunits in the Gleim materials that correspond to the CSOs' coverage.

The listing below contains the CSO areas covered by each section of the CPA exam with the AICPA percentage weighting for each CSO area. NOTE: The AICPA provides ranges, e.g., 17 to 23%. We averaged each range to a single number, e.g., 20%.

Auditing and Attestation

I. Engagement Acceptance and Understanding the Assignment	14%
II. Understanding the Entity and Its Environment (including Internal Control)	18%
III. Performing Audit Procedures and Evaluating Evidence	18%
IV. Evaluating Audit Findings, Communications, and Reporting	18%
V. Accounting and Review Services Engagements	14%
VI. Professional Responsibilities	18%
	100%

Business Environment and Concepts

I. Corporate Governance	18%
II. Economic Concepts and Analysis	18%
III. Financial Management	21%
IV. Information Systems and Communications	17%
V. Strategic Planning	12%
VI. Operations Management	14%
	100%

Financial Accounting and Reporting

I. Conceptual Framework, Standards, Standard Setting, and Presentation of Financial Statements	20%
II. Financial Statement Accounts: Recognition, Measurement, Valuation, Calculation, Presentation, and Disclosures	30%
III. Specific Transactions, Events and Disclosures: Recognition, Measurement, Valuation, Calculation, Presentation, and Disclosures	30%
IV. Governmental Accounting and Reporting	10%
V. Not-for-Profit (Nongovernmental) Accounting and Reporting	10%
	100%

Regulation

I. Ethics, Professional, and Legal Responsibilities	17%
II. Business Law	19%
III. Federal Tax Process, Procedures, Accounting, and Planning	13%
IV. Federal Taxation of Property Transactions	14%
V. Federal Taxation of Individuals	16%
VI. Federal Taxation of Entities	21%
	100%

Your authors have divided the overall task of preparing for the CPA exam into 20 study units for each section of the exam. As you will see in the Study Unit 2 cross-references, these study units conform to (or parallel) the AICPA CSOs. Note that the scope of most AICPA areas is broad, resulting in coverage by more than one Gleim study unit. The Gleim *CPA Review* books have AICPA CSO/Gleim study unit cross-references listed in an appendix so that you are assured of being completely prepared to PASS.

1.8 WHEN TO TAKE THE EXAM

The CPA exam should be taken immediately after graduation (or while in the last semester of school, if permitted) while your education is still fresh. If you take the exam before taking all relevant accounting and business law courses, you will have to study (rather than review) the relevant subject matter. Courses relevant to the CPA exam include

- Intermediate Financial Accounting
- Advanced Financial Accounting
- Governmental and Not-for-Profit Accounting (may be part of Advanced Financial Accounting)
- Economics and Finance
- Federal Tax: Individual, Partnership, Corporate, and Estate & Gift
- Auditing
- Accounting (Information) Systems
- Cost and Managerial Accounting
- Business Law

Out of the 55 U.S. jurisdictions, 54 have implemented the "150-hour rule," which requires a bachelor's degree plus 30 hours to be certified. Only the U.S. Virgin Islands have not passed this requirement. At the time of publication of the 2015 edition, the 150-hour rule is effective for all jurisdictions except Colorado. It becomes effective in Colorado on July 1, 2015.

Thirty-five of the states and jurisdictions that have implemented the 150-hour rule allow candidates to sit for the exam before completing 150 hours:

Alaska	Florida	Maine	New Jersey	Utah
Arizona	Georgia	Maryland	New Mexico	Vermont
Arkansas	Guam	Massachusetts	New York	Virgin Islands*
California	Hawaii	Michigan	North Carolina	Virginia
Colorado	Idaho	Minnesota*	Pennsylvania**	Washington, DC
Connecticut	Iowa	Montana	Rhode Island	West Virginia
Delaware	Kentucky	New Hampshire	South Carolina	Wisconsin

* Requires residency or employment in this jurisdiction to take the exam there.
** Pennsylvania is still an optional 150-hour state but requires 150 hours for licensure.

If you have already graduated and have not signed up to take the CPA exam, do so as soon as possible and start studying.

1.9 WHERE TO TAKE THE EXAM

An important consideration in deciding where to take the exam is continuing professional education (CPE) requirements. Most state boards require CPE to renew a license to practice. Many accountants take the CPA examination, obtain the experience necessary to become licensed to practice public accounting, subsequently leave public accounting, and do not maintain their CPE requirements. If you are **not** going to practice public accounting or do **not** need a license to practice public accounting, you may wish to sit for the CPA exam in a state that has a CPA certificate separate from its license to practice and where CPE requirements apply only to the license to practice.

Seven jurisdictions (Alabama, Connecticut, Hawaii, Kansas, Montana, Nebraska, and Oklahoma) issue CPA certificates that are separate from the license to practice. Some of these states do **not** require public accounting experience to receive the CPA certificate, do **not** require CPE of their CPA certificate holders, **and/or** do **not** require residency to sit for the CPA exam. Contact the individual state board for more information.

Go to www.gleim.com/states to access requirements for each Board of Accountancy. Then, call or check the website of the boards for those states in which you may want to be certified. Communicate your intentions and confirm your expectations in writing, i.e., separate CPA certificate, no experience required for CPA certificate, residency not required, CPE not required of certificate holders, etc.

1.10 PASS RATES

Pass Rates on the CPA Exam*

	Candidates		
	2012	2013	2014 (Q1 and Q2)**
AUD	46.9	45.9	48.3
BEC	52.8	55.8	55.9
FAR	48.0	48.3	46.0
REG	42.2	48.5	50.5

*Both domestic and international pass rates are included.
**Pass rates for Q3 and Q4 had not yet been released at time of printing.

For more recent pass rates, check our website at www.gleim.com/CPAPassRates.

The implication of these pass rates for you as a CPA candidate is that you have to be, on average, in the top 45% of all candidates to pass. A major difference among CPA candidates is their preparation program. You have access to the best CPA review material; it is up to you to use it. Conversely, if you do not apply the suggestions in this booklet, you will be at a disadvantage to the tens of thousands of candidates who pass with Gleim. Even if you are enrolled in a review course that uses other manuals, you will benefit with the Gleim Premium CPA Review System.

1.11 EXAM COSTS

Cost estimates, which vary from state to state, appear below. Some states offer lower fees if you apply for all four sections at the same time. However, note that in most states, your NTS expires after 6 months. You should only apply for those sections you plan to take within the next 6 months. To determine your current State Board fee, see www.gleim.com/states.

	Auditing	Business	Financial	Regulation	TOTAL
NASBA	$ 18.00	$ 18.00	$ 18.00	$ 18.00	$ 72.00
AICPA	90.00	90.00	90.00	90.00	360.00
Prometric	82.35	63.25	82.35	63.25	291.20
Picture Fee	5.95	5.95	5.95	5.95	23.80
Subtotal	$196.30	$177.20	$196.30	$177.20	$747.00
State Board Fees	??	??	??	??	??
Total Costs	??	??	??	??	??

1.12 THE GLEIM SYSTEM FOR CPA SUCCESS

The following is an abbreviated description of the information that is covered throughout the rest of this booklet.

The Preparation Process -- In order to be successful on examinations, you need to

1. Become familiar with the exam process, including the exam's purpose, coverage, preparation methods, format, administration, grading, and pass rates
2. Conceptualize the subject matter tested
3. Perfect your question-answering techniques
4. Plan and practice exam execution
5. Develop the confidence you need to succeed!

1.13 STEPS TO BECOME A CPA

Once you have reviewed all of the information in Subunits 1.1 through 1.13, you are ready to begin taking the steps to become a CPA. Use the checkpoints below to keep yourself on track and to make sure you do not omit any important steps. If you would like, check off the boxes as you progress to give yourself a sense of accomplishment regarding the huge undertaking you have embarked upon.

1	Become knowledgeable about the exam and decide which section you will take first.
2	Purchase the Gleim Premium CPA Review System to thoroughly prepare for the CPA exam. Commit to our systematic preparation for the exam as described in our review materials, including this booklet.
3	Set up your Study Planner in Gleim Online to design a personalized study schedule that meets your needs. Then, communicate with your Personal Counselor to ensure you are studying effectively. Call (888) 874-5346 or email personalcounselor@gleim.com.
4	Determine the board of accountancy (i.e., state) to which you will apply to sit for the CPA exam (discussed in Subunit 1.9).
5	Obtain, complete, and submit your application form, including transcripts, fees, etc., to your State Board or NASBA. You should receive a Notice To Schedule (NTS) from NASBA in 4 to 6 weeks.

- A NTS is valid for a specific period established by the boards of accountancy. Only apply for the section(s) you will sit for during this time as you will forfeit your fees for sections not taken.

6	Schedule your test with Prometric (online or by calling your local Prometric testing site). Schedule **30 to 45 days before** the date you plan to sit for the exam.
7	Work systematically through the study units in each section of the Gleim Premium CPA Review System (*Auditing*, *Business*, *Financial*, and *Regulation*).
8	Sit for and PASS the CPA exam while you are in control, as described in Study Unit 6 of this booklet. Gleim Guarantees Success!
9	Enjoy your career and pursue multiple certifications (CIA, CMA, EA, etc.), recommend Gleim to others who are also taking these exams, and stay up-to-date on your continuing professional education with Gleim CPE. Additional certifications are appreciably easier to earn after recently passing the CPA exam, and they open many other doors of opportunity.

STUDY UNIT TWO
AICPA CONTENT SPECIFICATION OUTLINES
AND SKILL SPECIFICATION OUTLINES

(12 pages of outline)

2.1 OVERVIEW OF CSOs AND SSOs

This study unit contains the AICPA Content Specification Outlines (CSOs) and an overview of the Skill Specification Outlines (SSOs) for the CPA exam.

In the Uniform CPA Examination Alert newsletter of Spring 2009, when it was first unveiling the new CBT-e exam, the AICPA indicated that the content specification outlines have several purposes, including

1. *Ensure that the testing of entry-level knowledge and skills that are important to the protection of the public interest is consistent across examination administrations*

2. *Determine what kinds of questions should be included on the CPA Examination so that every version of the examination reflects the required distribution and balance of knowledge and skill components*

3. *Provide candidates preparing for the examination with information about the subject matter that is eligible to be tested*

The SSOs are universal for all four sections and disclose how different levels of skills are tested.

The Gleim **CPA Review System** is organized to ensure comprehensive coverage of the AICPA CSOs. On the following pages, we have provided cross-references to our study units and subunits alongside the CSOs to facilitate your studying process.

For the CSOs, the AICPA discloses the percentage coverage of each subject by "areas" only. Note that the AICPA "percentage coverage" is given in ranges, e.g., 17-23%. We present the midpoint of each range to simplify and provide more relevant information to CPA candidates, e.g., 20% instead of 17-23%. All Gleim presentations are simplified and more relevant to facilitate your study, learning, and success.

2.2 CSO: BUSINESS ENVIRONMENT AND CONCEPTS WITH GLEIM CROSS-REFERENCES

AICPA CONTENT SPECIFICATION OUTLINE

Business Environment and Concepts

I. **Corporate Governance (18%)**

    A.   Rights, Duties, Responsibilities, Authority, and Ethics of the Board of Directors, Officers, and Other Employees

        1.   Financial and non-financial reporting - 1.1

        2.   Internal control (including COSO or similar framework) - 1.2-1.3

        3.   Enterprise risk management (including COSO or similar framework) - 1.4

    B.   Entity-Level Controls - 1.3

        1.   Tone at the top – establishing control environment

        2.   Monitoring control effectiveness

        3.   Change control process

II. **Economic Concepts and Analysis (18%)**

    A.   Changes in Economic and Business Cycles – Economic Measures/Indicators - SU 2-SU 3

    B.   Globalization and Local Economies

        1.   Impacts of globalization on companies - 4.1, 4.3

        2.   Shifts in economic balance of power (e.g., capital) to/from developed from/to emerging markets - 4.2

    C.   Market Influences on Business Strategies - SU 2-SU 3

    D.   Financial Risk Management

        1.   Market, interest rate, currency, liquidity, credit, price, and other risks - 4.2, 5.1-5.3

        2.   Means for mitigating/controlling financial risks - 4.3, 5.4

III. **Financial Management (21%)**

    A.   Financial Modeling, Projections, and Analysis

        1.   Forecasting and trends - SU 6

        2.   Financial and risk analysis - 1.5, 8.2-8.3, 9.2-9.6

        3.   Impact of inflation/deflation - 3.5, 4.2

    B.   Financial Decisions

        1.   Debt, equity, leasing - 7.1-7.3

        2.   Asset and investment management - SU 5, SU 8

    C.   Capital Management, including Working Capital

        1.   Capital structure - 7.1-7.2, 7.4-7.5, 10.5

        2.   Short-term and long-term financing - 7.1-7.2, 8.1, 9.1

        3.   Asset effectiveness and/or efficiency - SU 8, SU 10

    D.   Financial Valuations (e.g., Fair Value)

        1.   Methods for calculating valuations - 5.3, 9.3, 10.3-10.5

        2.   Evaluating assumptions used in valuations - 5.3, 9.3-9.4, SU 10

    E.   Financial Transaction Processes and Controls - 11.2, 11.4

IV. **Information Systems and Communications (17%)**

    A.   Organizational Needs Assessment

        1.   Data capture - 11.1-11.3

        2.   Processing - 11.2-11.3

        3.   Reporting - 11.3

        4.   Role of information technology in business strategy - SU 11

    B.   Systems Design and Other Elements - 12.1-12.2

        1.   Business process design (integrated systems, automated, and manual interfaces) - 12.3-12.5

        2.   Information Technology (IT) control objectives - 14.1-14.4

        3.   Role of technology systems in control monitoring - 12.6, 14.1-14.4

        4.   Operational effectiveness - 14.1

        5.   Segregation of duties - 14.5

        6.   Policies - 14.1

    C.   Security - 13.4, 14.3

        1.   Technologies and security management features

        2.   Policies

    D.   Internet – Implications for Business

        1.   Electronic commerce - 13.2-13.4
        2.   Opportunities for business process reengineering - 12.5, 17.3
        3.   Roles of Internet evolution on business operations and organization cultures - SU 13

    E.   Types of Information System and Technology Risks - 12.1-12.4, 14.1

    F.   Disaster Recovery and Business Continuity - 12.6

V. **Strategic Planning (12%)**

    A.   Market and Risk Analysis - 15.1-15.2
    B.   Strategy Development, Implementation, and Monitoring - 15.1-15.2
    C.   Planning Techniques

        1.   Budget and analysis - 15.3-15.4, SU 16
        2.   Forecasting and projection - SU 6, SU 16
        3.   Coordinating information from various sources for integrated planning - 15.2, 16.1, 16.3

VI. **Operations Management (14%)**

    A.   Performance Management and Impact of Measures on Behavior

        1.   Financial and nonfinancial measures - 10.3-10.4, 17.2
        2.   Impact of marketing practices on performance - 15.1, 17.1-17.2
        3.   Incentive compensation - 17.2

    B.   Cost Measurement Methods and Techniques - SU 18-SU 20
    C.   Process Management

        1.   Approaches, techniques, measures, and benefits to process-management-driven businesses - 17.3

        2.   Roles of shared services, outsourcing, and off-shore operations, and their implications on business risks and controls - 17.3

        3.   Selecting and implementing improvement initiatives - 17.3-17.6

        4.   Business process reengineering - 17.3

        5.   Management philosophies and techniques for performance improvement such as Just in Time (JIT), Quality, Lean, Demand Flow, Theory of Constraints, and Six Sigma - 17.3

    D.   Project Management - 17.7

        1.   Project planning, implementation, and monitoring
        2.   Roles of project managers, project members, and oversight or steering groups
        3.   Project risks, including resource, scope, cost, and deliverables

2.3 CSO: AUDITING AND ATTESTATION WITH GLEIM CROSS-REFERENCES

AICPA CONTENT SPECIFICATION OUTLINE

Auditing and Attestation

I. **Engagement Acceptance and Understanding the Assignment (14%)**

    A.   Determine Nature and Scope of Engagement - 1.1-1.4

    B.   Consider the Firm's Policies and Procedures Pertaining to Client Acceptance and Continuance - 1.5

    C.   Communicate with the Predecessor Auditor - 3.1

    D.   Establish an Understanding with the Client and Document the Understanding Through an Engagement Letter or Other Written Communication with the Client - 3.1

    E.   Consider Other Planning Matters

        1.   Consider using the work of other independent auditors - 3.2, 17.1
        2.   Determine the extent of the involvement of professionals possessing specialized skills - 3.2, 4.2
        3.   Consider the independence, objectivity, and competency of the internal audit function - 4.1

    F.   Identify Matters Related to Planning and Prepare Documentation for Communications with Those Charged with Governance - 9.2

II.   **Understanding the Entity and Its Environment (including Internal Control) (18%)**

    A.   Determine and Document Materiality - 3.2-3.3

    B.   Conduct and Document Risk Assessment Discussions Among Audit Team, Concurrently with Discussion on Susceptibility of the Entity's Financial Statement to Material Misstatement Due to Fraud - 3.3

    C.   Consideration of Fraud - 3.6

        1.   Identify characteristics of fraud
        2.   Document required discussions regarding risk of fraud
        3.   Document inquiries of management about fraud
        4.   Identify and assess risks that may result in material misstatements due to fraud

    D.   Perform and Document Risk Assessment Procedures

        1.   Identify, conduct and document appropriate inquiries of management and others within the entity - 3.4

        2.   Perform appropriate analytical procedures to understand the entity and identify areas of risk - 3.5

        3.   Obtain information to support inquiries through observation and inspection (including reading corporate minutes, etc.) - 3.4

    E.   Consider Additional Aspects of the Entity and its Environment, including: Industry, Regulatory and Other External Factors; Strategies and Business Risks; Financial Performance - 3.4

    F.   Consider Internal Control

        1.   Perform procedures to assess the control environment, including consideration of the COSO framework and identifying entity-level controls - 5.1-5.4

        2.   Obtain and document an understanding of business processes and information flows - 5.1-5.4

        3.   Determine the effect of information technology on the effectiveness of an entity's internal control - 5.5

        4.   Perform risk assessment procedures to evaluate the design and implementation of internal controls relevant to an audit of financial statements - 5.3

        5.   Identify key risks associated with general controls in a financial IT environment - 5.5, 8.3

        6.   Identify key risks associated with application controls in a financial IT environment - 5.5, 6.4, 7.5, 8.3

        7.   Assess whether the entity has designed controls to mitigate key risks associated with general controls or application functionality - 5.5

        8.   Identify controls relevant to reliable financial reporting and the period-end financial reporting process - SU 6-SU 7

        9.   Consider limitations of internal control - 5.1

       10.   Consider the effects of service organizations on internal control - 9.4

       11.   Consider the risk of management override of internal controls - 3.6

    G.   Document an Understanding of the Entity and its Environment, including Each Component of the Entity's Internal Control, in Order to Assess Risks - 5.3-5.4

    H.   Assess and Document the Risk of Material Misstatements - SU 8

        1.   Identify and document financial statement assertions and formulate audit objectives including significant financial statement balances, classes of transactions, disclosures, and accounting estimates

        2.   Relate the identified risks to relevant assertions and consider whether the risks could result in a material misstatement to the financial statements

        3.   Assess and document the risk of material misstatement that relates to both financial statement level and specific assertions

        4.   Identify and document conditions and events that may indicate risks of material misstatement

    I.   Identify and Document Significant Risks that Require Special Audit Consideration

        1.   Significant recent economic, accounting, or other developments - 3.4
        2.   Related parties and related party transactions - 4.3
        3.   Improper revenue recognition - 3.4, 11.1
        4.   Nonroutine or complex transactions - 3.4
        5.   Significant accounting estimates - 4.4, 13.2
        6.   Noncompliance with laws and regulations including illegal acts - 3.7

III. Performing Audit Procedures and Evaluating Evidence (18%)

    A. Develop Overall Responses to Risks - 8.2

        1. Develop overall responses to risks identified and use the risks of material misstatement to drive the nature, timing, and extent of further audit procedures

        2. Document significant risks identified, related controls evaluated, and overall responses to address assessed risks

        3. Determine and document performance materiality/level(s) of tolerable misstatement

    B. Perform Audit Procedures Responsive to Risks of Material Misstatement; Obtain and Document Evidence to Form a Basis for Conclusions

        1. Design and perform audit procedures whose nature, timing, and extent are responsive to the assessed risk of material misstatement - 10.1

        2. Integrating audits: in an integrated audit of internal control over financial reporting and the financial statements, design and perform testing of controls to accomplish the objectives of both audits simultaneously - 9.3

        3. Design, perform, and document tests of controls to evaluate design effectiveness - 8.1, 9.3, 10.1

        4. Design, perform, and document tests of controls to evaluate operating effectiveness - 8.1, 9.3, 10.1

        5. Perform substantive procedures - SU 11-SU 13

        6. Perform audit sampling - SU 15

        7. Perform analytical procedures - 3.5

        8. Confirm balances and/or transactions with third parties - 10.2

        9. Examine inventories and other assets - 12.2, 13.1

        10. Perform other tests of details, balances, and journal entries - SU 11-SU 13

        11. Perform audit procedures on significant accounting estimates - 4.4

        12. Auditing fair value measurements and disclosures, including the use of specialists in evaluating estimates - 4.4

        13. Perform tests on unusual year-end transactions - SU 11-SU 13

        14. Audits performed in accordance with International Standards on Auditing (ISAs) or auditing standards of another country: determine if differences exist and whether additional audit procedures are required - Highlighted in each affected SU and summarized in Appendix A

        15. Evaluate contingencies - 14.1

        16. Obtain and evaluate lawyers' letters - 14.1

        17. Review subsequent events - 14.2

        18. Obtaining and placing reliance on representations from management - 14.3

        19. Identify material weaknesses, significant deficiencies, and other control deficiencies - 9.1

IV. Evaluating Audit Findings, Communications, and Reporting (18%)

    A. Perform Overall Analytical Procedures - 3.5

    B. Evaluate the Sufficiency and Appropriateness of Audit Evidence and Document Engagement Conclusions - 10.3

    C. Evaluate Whether Audit Documentation is in Accordance with Professional Standards - 10.3

    D. Review the Work Performed by Others, including Specialists and Other Auditors, to Provide Reasonable Assurance that Objectives are Achieved - 4.2, 17.1

    E. Document the Summary of Uncorrected Misstatements and Related Conclusions - 10.3

    F. Evaluate Whether Financial Statements are Free of Material Misstatements - 16.1

    G. Consider the Entity's Ability to Continue as a Going Concern - 14.4, 17.3

    H. Consider Other Information in Documents Containing Audited Financial Statements (e.g., Supplemental Information and Management's Discussion and Analysis) - 18.1-18.7

    I. Retain Audit Documentation as Required by Standards and Regulations - 10.3

    J.   Prepare Communications

        1.   Reports on audited financial statements - SU 16-SU 17
        2.   Reports required by government auditing standards - SU 20
        3.   Reports on compliance with laws and regulations - 19.7
        4.   Reports on internal control - 9.3
        5.   Reports on the processing of transactions by service organizations - 9.4
        6.   Reports on agreed-upon procedures - 19.4
        7.   Reports on financial forecasts and projections - 19.5
        8.   Reports on pro forma financial information - 19.6
        9.   Special reports - 18.8-18.11
      10.   Reissue reports - 14.2, 17.4
      11.   Communicate internal control related matters identified in the audit - 9.1
      12.   Communications with those charged with governance - 9.2
      13.   Subsequent discovery of facts existing at the date of the auditor's report - 14.2
      14.   Consideration after the report date of omitted procedures - 4.5

V.   **Accounting and Review Services Engagements (14%)**

    A.   Plan the Engagement

        1.   Determine nature and scope of engagement - 19.1-19.2

        2.   Decide whether to accept or continue the client and engagement including determining the appropriateness of the engagement to meet the client's needs and consideration of independence standards - 19.1-19.2

        3.   Establish an understanding with the client and document the understanding through an engagement letter or other written communication with the client - 19.1-19.2

        4.   Consider change in engagement - 19.3

        5.   Determine if reports are to be used by third parties - 19.1-19.2

    B.   Obtain and Document Evidence to Form a Basis for Conclusions

        1.   Obtain an understanding of the client's operations, business, and industry - 19.1-19.2

        2.   Obtain knowledge of accounting principles and practices in the industry and the client - 19.1-19.2

        3.   Perform analytical procedures for review services - 19.2

        4.   Obtain representations from management for review services - 19.2

        5.   Perform other engagement procedures - 19.1-19.2

        6.   Consider departures from generally accepted accounting principles (GAAP) or other comprehensive basis of accounting (OCBOA) - 19.1-19.2

        7.   Prepare documentation from evidence gathered - 19.1-19.2

        8.   Retain documentation as required by standards - 19.1-19.2

        9.   Review the work performed to provide reasonable assurance that objectives are achieved - 19.1-19.2

    C.   Prepare Communications

        1.   Reports on compilations - 19.1-19.3
        2.   Reports on reviews - 19.2-19.3
        3.   Restricted use of reports - 19.1-19.3
        4.   Communicating to management and others - 19.1-19.3
        5.   Subsequent discovery of facts existing at the date of the report - 19.1-19.3
        6.   Consider degree of responsibility for supplementary information - 19.1-19.3

VI.   **Professional Responsibilities (18%)**

    A.   Ethics and Independence

        1.   Code of Professional Conduct (AICPA) - 2.1-2.6

        2.   Requirements related to issuers, including the PCAOB, the SEC and the Sarbanes-Oxley Act of 2002, Titles II and III, Section 303 - 2.7

        3.   Government Accountability Office (GAO) - 20.1

        4.   Department of Labor (DOL) - 2.7

        5.   Code of Ethics for Professional Accountants (IFAC) - 2.7

    B.   Other Professional Responsibilities

        1.   A firm's system of quality control - 1.5

        2.   General role, structure, and requirements of the PCAOB (Title I and Title IV of the Sarbanes-Oxley Act of 2002) - 2.7

2.4 CSO: REGULATION WITH GLEIM CROSS-REFERENCES

AICPA CONTENT SPECIFICATION OUTLINE

Regulation

I. **Ethics, Professional, and Legal Responsibilities (17%)**

    A.   Ethics and Responsibilities in Tax Practice

        1.   Treasury Department Circular 230 - 1.1

        2.   AICPA Statements on Standards for Tax Services - 1.2

        3.   Internal Revenue Code of 1986, as amended, and Regulations related to tax return preparers - 1.3

    B.   Licensing and Disciplinary Systems - 1.4

        1.   Role of state boards of accountancy

        2.   Requirements of regulatory agencies

    C.   Legal Duties and Responsibilities

        1.   Common law duties and liability to clients and third parties - 2.4

        2.   Federal statutory liability - 2.3

        3.   Privileged communications, confidentiality, and privacy acts - 2.5

II. **Business Law (19%)**

    A.   Agency

        1.   Formation and termination - 16.1, 16.4

        2.   Authority of agents and principals - 16.2-16.3

        3.   Duties and liabilities of agents and principals - 16.2-16.3

    B.   Contracts

        1.   Formation - 17.1-17.8

        2.   Performance - 17.9

        3.   Third party assignments - 17.11-17.12

        4.   Discharge, breach, and remedies - 17.9-17.10

    C.   Uniform Commercial Code

        1.   Sales contracts - 18.1-18.6

        2.   Negotiable instruments - SU 19

        3.   Secured transactions - 18.7-18.10

        4.   Documents of title and title transfer - 19.7

    D.   Debtor-Creditor Relationships

        1.   Rights, duties, and liabilities of debtors, creditors, and guarantors - 18.10, 20.1-20.2, 20.6

        2.   Bankruptcy and insolvency - 20.3-20.5

    E.   Government Regulation of Business

        1.   Federal securities regulation - 2.1-2.2

        2.   Other federal laws and regulations (antitrust, copyright, patents, money-laundering, labor, employment, and ERISA) - 16.5-16.8

    F.   Business Structure (Selection of a Business Entity) - SU 14-SU 15

        1.   Advantages, disadvantages, implications, and constraints

        2.   Formation, operation, and termination

        3.   Financial structure, capitalization, profit and loss allocation, and distributions

        4.   Rights, duties, legal obligations, and authority of owners and management

III. **Federal Tax Process, Procedures, Accounting, and Planning (13%)**

    A.   Federal Tax Legislative Process - 13.1

    B.   Federal Tax Procedures - 13.2

        1.   Due dates and related extensions of time

        2.   Internal Revenue Service (IRS) audit and appeals process

        3.   Judicial process

        4.   Required disclosure of tax return positions

        5.   Substantiation requirements

        6.   Penalties

        7.   Statute of limitations

    C.   Accounting Periods - 3.3, 7.1, 10.1, 11.1

D.   Accounting Methods

1.   Recognition of revenues and expenses under cash, accrual, or other permitted methods - 3.3-3.5, 6.1, 7.1-7.3, 13.4

2.   Inventory valuation methods, including uniform capitalization rules - 13.4

3.   Accounting for long-term contracts - 13.4

4.   Installment sales - 6.5

E.   Tax Return Elections, Including Federal Status Elections, Alternative Treatment Elections, or Other Types of Elections Applicable to an Individual or Entity's Tax Return - 3.1, 7.1, 10.1, 11.1

F.   Tax Planning - SU 5, SU 8, 13.3

1.   Alternative treatments
2.   Projections of tax consequences
3.   Implications of different business entities
4.   Impact of proposed tax audit adjustments
5.   Impact of estimated tax payment rules on planning
6.   Role of taxes in decision-making

G.   Impact of Multijurisdictional Tax Issues on Federal Taxation (Including Consideration of Local, State, and Multinational Tax Issues) - 13.5

H.   Tax Research and Communication - 13.1

1.   Authoritative hierarchy
2.   Communications with or on behalf of clients

IV.   Federal Taxation of Property Transactions (14%)

A.   Types of Assets - 6.1, 6.3, 6.5
B.   Basis and Holding Periods of Assets - 6.1, 6.3
C.   Cost Recovery (Depreciation, Depletion, and Amortization) - 6.2
D.   Taxable and Nontaxable Sales and Exchanges - 6.4. 6.6
E.   Amount and Character of Gains and Losses, and Netting Process - 6.3, 6.7
F.   Related Party Transactions - 6.4
G.   Estate and Gift Taxation

1.   Transfers subject to the gift tax - 12.3, 12.5
2.   Annual exclusion and gift tax deductions - 12.3
3.   Determination of taxable estate - 12.4
4.   Marital deduction - 12.3-12.4
5.   Unified credit - 12.4

V.   Federal Taxation of Individuals (16%)

A.   Gross Income - 3.3-3.5

1.   Inclusions and exclusions
2.   Characterization of income

B.   Reporting of Items from Pass-Through Entities - 10.3, 11.1-11.5

C.   Adjustments and Deductions to Arrive at Taxable Income - SU 4-SU 5

D.   Passive Activity Losses - 5.5

E.   Loss Limitations - 5.5

F.   Taxation of Retirement Plan Benefits - 3.5

G.   Filing Status and Exemptions - 3.1-3.2

H.   Tax Computations and Credits - 5.1-5.3

I.   Alternative Minimum Tax - 5.4

VI.   Federal Taxation of Entities (21%)

A.   Similarities and Distinctions in Tax Treatment Among Business Entities

1.   Formation - 7.1, 9.1, 10.1, 11.1, 11.7
2.   Operation - 7.2-7.5, 10.2, 11.3-11.4
3.   Distributions - 9.2, 10.3, 11.5
4.   Liquidation - 9.4-9.7, 10.1, 11.6

B.   Differences Between Tax and Financial Accounting - 7.5

1.   Reconciliation of book income to taxable income
2.   Disclosures under Schedule M-3

C. C Corporations

    1. Determination of taxable income/loss - 7.2-7.4
    2. Tax computations and credits, including alternative minimum tax - 8.1-8.2, 8.5-8.8
    3. Net operating losses - 7.4
    4. Entity/owner transactions, including contributions and distributions - 9.1-9.3, 9.8-9.9
    5. Earnings and profits - 7.3, 8.7
    6. Consolidated returns - 8.3-8.4

D. S Corporations

    1. Eligibility and election - 10.1
    2. Determination of ordinary income/loss and separately stated items - 10.2
    3. Basis of shareholders' interest - 10.2
    4. Entity/owner transactions, including contributions and distributions - 10.3
    5. Built-in gains tax - 10.4

E. Partnerships

    1. Determination of ordinary income/loss and separately stated items - 11.1-11.2
    2. Basis of partner's/member's interest and basis of assets contributed to the partnership - 11.1-11.3
    3. Partnership and partner elections - 11.1-11.2
    4. Transactions between a partner and the partnership - 11.3
    5. Treatment of partnership liabilities - 11.4
    6. Distribution of partnership assets - 11.5
    7. Ownership changes and liquidation and termination of partnership - 11.1-11.2, 11.6

F. Trusts and Estates

    1. Types of trusts - 12.1
    2. Income and deductions - 12.1
    3. Determination of beneficiary's share of taxable income - 12.2

G. Tax-Exempt Organizations - 11.8

    1. Types of organizations
    2. Obtaining and maintaining tax-exempt status
    3. Unrelated business income

2.5 CSO: FINANCIAL ACCOUNTING AND REPORTING WITH GLEIM CROSS-REFERENCES

AICPA CONTENT SPECIFICATION OUTLINE

Financial Accounting and Reporting

I. **Conceptual Framework, Standards, Standard Setting, and Presentation of Financial Statements (20%)**

    A. Process by which Accounting Standards are Set and Roles of Accounting Standard-Setting Bodies - 1.1

        1. U.S. Securities and Exchange Commission (SEC)
        2. Financial Accounting Standards Board (FASB)
        3. International Accounting Standards Board (IASB)
        4. Governmental Accounting Standards Board (GASB)

    B. Conceptual Framework - 1.2-1.9

        1. Financial reporting by business entities - 1.2
        2. Financial reporting by not-for-profit (nongovernmental) entities - 1.3
        3. Financial reporting by state and local governmental entities - 1.4

    C. Financial Reporting, Presentation, and Disclosures in General-Purpose Financial Statements

        1. Balance sheet/Statement of financial position - 2.1
        2. Income statement/Statement of profit or loss - 2.2
        3. Statement of comprehensive income - 2.3
        4. Statement of changes in equity - 2.4
        5. Statement of cash flows - SU 17
        6. Notes to financial statements - 1.7, 4.1, 4.7
        7. Consolidated and combined financial statements - SU 15

    D. SEC Reporting Requirements (e.g., Form 10-Q, 10-K) - 1.10

    E. Other Financial Statement Presentations

        1. Personal financial statements - 2.5
        2. Financial statements of employee benefit plans/trusts - SU 11
        3. Liquidation basis financial statements - 1.8

    F.   Special Purpose Frameworks

        1.   Cash basis - 2.5
        2.   Modified cash basis - 2.5
        3.   Income tax basis - 2.5

II. **Financial Statement Accounts: Recognition, Measurement, Valuation, Calculation, Presentation, and Disclosures (30%)**

    A.   Cash and Cash Equivalents - 5.1

    B.   Receivables - SU 6

    C.   Inventory - SU 7

    D.   Property, Plant, and Equipment - SU 8

    E.   Investments - 5.6

        1.   Financial assets at fair value through profit or loss - 5.2-5.3
        2.   Available for sale financial assets - 5.3
        3.   Held-to-maturity investments - 5.3
        4.   Joint ventures - 5.4
        5.   Equity method investments (investments in associates) - 5.4
        6.   Investment property - 8.1

    F.   Intangible Assets – Goodwill and Other - SU 9

    G.   Payables and Accrued Liabilities - 10.1-10.6

    H.   Deferred Revenue - 10.4

    I.   Long-Term Debt (Financial Liabilities)

        1.   Notes payable - 12.9
        2.   Bonds payable - 12.1-12.4
        3.   Debt with conversion features and other options - 12.6
        4.   Modifications and extinguishments - 12.7-12.8
        5.   Troubled debt restructurings by debtors - 12.10
        6.   Debt covenant compliance - 2.1

    J.   Equity - SU 14

    K.   Revenue Recognition - 3.5-3.6

    L.   Costs and Expenses - 2.2

    M.   Compensation and Benefits - SU 11

        1.   Compensated absences
        2.   Deferred compensation arrangements
        3.   Nonretirement postemployment benefits
        4.   Retirement benefits
        5.   Stock compensation (share-based payments)

    N.   Income Taxes - 10.7-10.11

III. **Specific Transactions, Events, and Disclosures: Recognition, Measurement, Valuation, Calculation, Presentation, and Disclosures (30%)**

    A.   Accounting Changes and Error Corrections - 3.3

    B.   Asset Retirement and Environmental Obligations - 12.11-12.12

    C.   Business Combinations - 15.1

    D.   Consolidation (including Off-Balance Sheet Transactions, Variable-Interest Entities and Noncontrolling Interests) - 15.2-15.6

    E.   Contingencies, Commitments, and Guarantees (Provisions) - 13.8-13.9

    F.   Earnings Per Share - 3.4

    G.   Exit or Disposal Activities and Discontinued Operations - 3.1

    H.   Extraordinary and Unusual Items - 3.2

    I.   Fair Value Measurements, Disclosures, and Reporting - 3.7

    J.   Derivatives and Hedge Accounting - 16.1

    K.   Foreign Currency Transactions and Translation - 16.2

    L.   Impairment - 8.8

    M.   Interim Financial Reporting - 4.3

    N.   Leases - 13.1-13.7

    O.   Distinguishing Liabilities from Equity - 12.6

    P.   Nonmonetary Transactions (Barter Transactions) - 8.6

    Q.   Related Parties and Related Party Transactions - 4.4

    R.   Research and Development Costs - 9.5

    S.   Risks and Uncertainties - 4.5

    T.   Segment Reporting - 4.2

    U.   Software Costs - 9.6

    V.   Subsequent Events - 4.6

    W.   Transfers and Servicing of Financial Assets and Derecognition - 6.3

IV. **Governmental Accounting and Reporting (10%)**

    A.   Governmental Accounting Concepts

        1.   Measurement focus and basis of accounting - 18.2
        2.   Fund accounting concepts and applications - 18.1-18.2
        3.   Budgetary accounting - 18.3-18.4

    B.   Format and Content of Comprehensive Annual Financial Report (CAFR)

        1.   Government-wide financial statements - 19.2
        2.   Governmental funds financial statements - 19.3
        3.   Proprietary funds financial statements - 19.4
        4.   Fiduciary funds financial statements - 19.5
        5.   Notes to financial statements - 19.1
        6.   Management's discussion and analysis - 19.1
        7.   Required supplementary information (RSI) other than Management's Discussion and Analysis - 19.1
        8.   Combining statements and individual fund statements and schedules - 19.1
        9.   Deriving government-wide financial statements and reconciliation requirements - 19.2-19.3

    C.   Financial Reporting Entity, Including Blended and Discrete Component Units - 19.1

    D.   Typical Items and Specific Types of Transactions and Events: Recognition, Measurement, Valuation, Calculation, and Presentation in Governmental Entity Financial Statements

        1.   Net position and components thereof - 19.2
        2.   Fund balances and components thereof - 18.3
        3.   Capital assets and infrastructure assets - 18.2, 18.7
        4.   General long-term liabilities - 18.2
        5.   Interfund activity, including transfers - 18.6
        6.   Nonexchange revenue transactions - 18.5
        7.   Expenditures - 18.2
        8.   Special items - 19.2-19.3
        9.   Encumbrances - 18.4

    E.   Accounting and Reporting for Governmental Not-for-Profit Organizations - SU 18-SU 19

V. **Not-for-Profit (Nongovernmental) Accounting and Reporting (10%)**

    A.   Financial Statements - 20.1

        1.   Statement of financial position
        2.   Statement of activities
        3.   Statement of cash flows
        4.   Statement of functional expenses

    B.   Typical Items and Specific Types of Transactions and Events: Recognition, Measurement, Valuation, Calculation, and Presentation in Financial Statements of Not-for-Profit Organizations - 20.4

        1.   Support, revenues, and contributions - 20.2
        2.   Types of restrictions on resources - 20.1-20.2
        3.   Types of net assets - 20.1
        4.   Expenses, including depreciation and functional expenses - 20.1
        5.   Investments - 20.3

2.6 SSOs

The SSOs identify the skills that will be tested on the CPA exam. The following table is based on information from the AICPA's *Candidate Bulletin* and explains the skills tested, weights assigned to each skill category (i.e., percentage of the total test score), question format that will be used to test the skill, and resources that will be available to the candidates to demonstrate proficiency in each skill.

Skills Category	Weight in AUD, FAR, REG	Weight in BEC	Question Format	Resource(s)
Knowledge and Understanding	60%	85%	Multiple-choice questions	Calculator
Application of the Body of Knowledge	40%	--	Task-Based Simulations	Authoritative literature, calculator, spreadsheets, etc.
Written Communication	--	15%	Written Communication Scenarios	Word processor with spell check

STUDY UNIT THREE
CONTENT PREPARATION, TEST ADMINISTRATION, AND PERFORMANCE GRADING

(5 pages of outline)

This study unit consists primarily of a detailed listing of procedures and rules used to administer the exam. Remember, the more you know about the examination process and what to expect, the greater your competitive advantage over others taking the exam. Leave nothing to chance, and be in total control of the examination process.

3.1 THE NONDISCLOSED EXAM

The AICPA is a nondisclosed exam for three stated reasons:

1. Pretest objective items (i.e., questions) to assemble a large, high-quality item bank
2. Statistically equate each examination for differences in the level of difficulty
3. Facilitate computer administration of the Uniform CPA Examination in the future

All candidates are required to accept the attestation that appears on the next page and are warned about the disastrous consequences of disclosing information about specific questions and/or answers.

Because the exam questions are not released to the public, we depend on feedback from CPAs and CPA candidates to know how to improve our materials, with emphasis on topics to be strengthened and/or added. Go to www.gleim.com/feedbackCPA or email your Personal Counselor with any of this kind of feedback. This process has been approved by the AICPA.

Based on candidate feedback, the Gleim CPA materials emphasize knowing exactly what will be expected of you during the CPA exam and preparing you for what will be required. We also help you avoid overpreparation. We change our approach and subject matter coverage as the exam changes.

3.2 THE AICPA CONFIDENTIALITY STATEMENT

As part of the AICPA's nondisclosure policy and to prove each candidate's willingness to adhere to this policy, a confidentiality and nondisclosure statement must be accepted by each candidate before each section is taken. This statement is reproduced here to remind all CPA candidates about the AICPA's strict policy of nondisclosure, which Gleim consistently supports and upholds.

"Please read the Confidentiality and Break Policy Statement presented below. You must accept the terms and conditions to proceed.

Policy Statement and Agreement Regarding Exam Confidentiality and the Taking of Breaks

I hereby agree that I will maintain the confidentiality of the Uniform CPA Examination. In addition, I agree that I will not:

- Divulge the nature or content of any Uniform CPA Examination question or answer under any circumstance
- Engage in any unauthorized communication during testing
- Refer to unauthorized materials or use unauthorized equipment during testing; or
- Remove or attempt to remove any Uniform CPA Examination materials, notes, or any other items from the examination room.

I understand and agree that liability for test administration activities, including but not limited to the adequacy or accuracy of test materials and equipment, and the accuracy of scoring and score reporting, will be limited to score correction or test retake at no additional fee. I waive any and all right to all other claims.

I further agree to report to the AICPA any examination question disclosures, or solicitations for disclosure of which I become aware.

I affirm that I have had the opportunity to read the Candidate Bulletin and I agree to all of its terms and conditions.

I understand that breaks are only allowed between testlets. I understand that I will be asked to complete any open testlet before leaving the testing room for a break.

In addition, I understand that failure to comply with this Policy Statement and Agreement may result in the invalidation of my grades, disqualification from future examinations, expulsion from the testing facility and possible civil or criminal penalties."

3.3 AICPA BOARD OF EXAMINERS (BOE)

The BOE sets policy for the Uniform CPA Examination using the legal and psychometric standards appropriate for licensure examinations. The BOE also oversees the development and scoring of the CPA exam.

There are three subcommittees that report to the Board: Content, Psychometric Oversight, and State Board. The Content Committee is responsible for the technical content of the CPA exam. The Psychometric Oversight Committee directs and evaluates CPA exam research and oversees the application of psychometric procedures. The State Board Committee links the BOE to state boards of accountancy by communicating state board concerns to the BOE and keeping the BOE advised of activities and decisions.

The AICPA Examinations Team, located in the AICPA's Ewing, New Jersey, office, carries out the Board policies. It is responsible for creating, delivering, and grading the Uniform CPA Examination.

Additional information about the Uniform CPA Examination, the Board of Examiners, and the Examinations Team is available at the AICPA's website (www.aicpa.org).

The Board of Examiners provides advance disclosure of changes to the CPA exam. This policy has resulted in increased confidence in and respect for the CPA exam from CPA candidates, academia, the profession, testing experts, and the general public.

3.4 HOW THE CPA EXAM IS PREPARED

The AICPA has contracted with third parties to produce vast quantities of multiple-choice questions, simulation tasks, and written communications. Only a qualified selection will be used, however, as the psychometric qualities of question testlets and exam versions will have to be carefully measured to grade and score each exam equitably on a comparative basis.

Implications for CPA candidates: Your CPA exam should be made up of questions so coverage follows the AICPA Content Specification Outlines. When taking the exam, your concern is with answering each question to the best of your ability, not with the topical coverage. Expect the unexpected and adjust. The more difficult the exam, the better for you because you will be better prepared to maximize your score. Remember, only the top 45% of CPA candidates PASS!

3.5 WHICH TAX LAW AND AUTHORITATIVE PRONOUNCEMENTS ARE TESTED?

Per the AICPA, accounting and auditing pronouncements are eligible to be tested on the Uniform CPA Examination in the testing window *beginning 6 months after a pronouncement's effective date*, unless early application is permitted. When early application is permitted, the new pronouncement is eligible to be tested in the window beginning *6 months after the issuance date*. In this case, both the old and new pronouncements may be tested until the old pronouncement is superseded.

Changes in the federal taxation area, the Internal Revenue Code, and federal taxation regulations may be included in the testing window beginning 6 months after the change's effective date or enactment date, whichever is later.

For all other subjects covered in the Regulation and Business Environment and Concepts sections, materials eligible to be tested include federal laws in the window beginning *6 months after their effective date* and uniform acts in the window beginning *1 year after their adoption by a simple majority of jurisdictions.*

The AICPA does not appear to be completely committed to the 6-month rule. For example, tax forms (if they appear in simulations) could be recent prior-year forms. Do NOT be distracted by the year; complete the form to the best of your ability. If a question on your exam provides an out-of-date tax rate, use that rate. Also, auditing, financial, and tax research databases are updated on the AICPA's schedule and may appear out of date. According to the Candidate Bulletin, candidates should use the research database as presented, even if a recent change to the literature is not yet appearing.

3.6 ADMINISTRATION OF THE CPA EXAM AT PROMETRIC

Prometric Testing Services has contracted with the AICPA and NASBA to deliver the CPA exam to CPA candidates at hundreds of testing centers throughout the U.S. and overseas. Prometric will schedule and administer your exam at one of the testing centers, reporting your responses back to the AICPA for grading.

3.7 PRETEST QUESTIONS

The multiple-choice questions within each test section are administered to candidates in three groups (called "testlets"). Each testlet contains "operational" and "pretest" questions. The operational questions are the ones used to generate the candidates' scores. Pretest questions are not scored; instead, candidates' responses to these questions are used to evaluate whether they should appear on future exams. Since you will not know which questions are operational versus pretest, you should answer every question as if it is an operational question.

The same is true regarding task-based simulation questions and written communications. The AICPA has announced, for example, that one of the three written communications will be a pretest, while the other two will be graded.

3.8 GRADING

The multiple-choice testlets have two levels of difficulty. Because of levels of difficulty, the CPA exam has become an adaptive exam. The scoring procedures take the statistical difficulty of the testlet into account so that candidates are scored fairly regardless of the difficulty of the testlets they take*. What does this mean for you as a candidate? Nothing. You still need to answer every question to the best of your ability.

Only correct responses are counted. In other words, there is NO PENALTY for incorrect responses that may occur from guessing. Accordingly, you want to maximize your potential total score by answering EVERY question. Study Unit 4, Subunit 6, "Educated Guessing," on page 31 has more information on this subject.

CPA exam scores are reported on a scale that runs from 0 to 99. A total score of 75 is required to pass each section. The total score is not a "percent correct" score. That is, your score is an indication of overall examination performance. The AICPA uses a specialized scoring method that takes into account the difficulty level and statistical properties of the questions you are given. Therefore, the passing score of 75 does not mean that you answered 75% of the questions correctly.

The total score is a combination of scores from the multiple-choice, simulation, and written communication portions of the exam. See the table below for the coverage breakdown details. There are no minimum scores required on the different kinds of questions or on different content areas within each section to earn a passing score.

	AUD-FAR-REG	BEC
Multiple-Choice	60%	85%
Task-Based Simulations	40%	N/A
Written Communication	N/A	15%

Relative Weight Assigned to Exam Portions (per AICPA's *Candidate Bulletin*)

---

* **CAUTION:** You may encounter an AICPA diagram that depicts how question difficulty is handled in the exam administration and grading process. We elected not to reproduce it here because it has NO value for you, the CPA candidate. The bottom line is that your focus is to answer EVERY question to the best of your ability and NOT concern yourself with matters regarding question difficulty. Again, the AICPA scoring procedures take the statistical difficulty of each question into account so that each CPA candidate is scored fairly.

Written Communication Grading

The grading for BEC's written communication is different than for any other testlet on the exam. Your responses are forwarded to contract graders who grade writing style.

In a written communication response, you will be graded on both technical content and writing skills, based on the following three criteria: organization, development, and expression. Study Unit 5, Subunit 6, contains more information on how to craft a response that will receive the highest score.

3.9 SCORE RELEASE

Below is a table of the AICPA's estimated score release schedule. Updated score release timelines will be announced every quarter on the AICPA's website. The release dates are targets, not guarantees, though the majority of scores will be released on the target date, according to the AICPA.

We have included target dates for the last quarter of 2014 as an example. For updated 2015 dates, which were not available at the time of print, check back at www.gleim.com/CPAscores. We will update the score release table as soon as that information is released.

AICPA Score Release Schedule

Results Received By*	Target Release Date Timeline	Target Score Release
October 20	11 business days following the cut-off receipt date	November 4
November 14	6 business days following the cut-off receipt date	November 24
December 1	6 business days following the cut-off receipt date	December 9
After December 1	6 business days after receiving all remaining scoring data for the testing window	December 18
*NOTE: "Results received by" refers to the date AICPA receives the test result, not the test date. Additionally, some candidates who take the BEC section might receive their scores approximately 1 week following the target release date due to additional analysis that might be required for the written communication tasks. Scores are generally released during regular business hours.		

3.10 RE-SCORE AND APPEAL PROCESSES

Virtually no grades are changed as a result of re-scoring and appealing. Be positive. We have a System for Success to get you through the exam. If you have to retake a section, move on and learn from your mistakes by studying your Candidate Performance Report (discussed in Study Unit 6, Subunit 10) and recommitting yourself to following our suggested study steps (discussed in Study Unit 6, Subunit 7).

STUDY UNIT FOUR
MULTIPLE-CHOICE QUESTIONS

(6 pages of outline)

This study unit and Study Unit 5 ("Task-Based Simulations and Written Communications") explain the question formats that appear on the CPA exam. We also explain how they are graded and suggest question-answering and time allocation techniques for each question format.

You will probably recognize that your question-answering technique is a specific control system application. We cannot say that your question-answering technique control system is *more* important than your other control systems, which include understanding the exam, studying individual Gleim study units, and planning and practicing exam execution. You will, however, be confident about your performance on the exam when you are poised to maximize your points on every question.

4.1 MULTIPLE-CHOICE TESTLETS

Each section of the CPA exam has three testlets of multiple-choice questions. They will be the first three testlets in every section. In AUD and FAR, each testlet will have 30 questions. In BEC and REG, each testlet will contain only 24 questions.

4.2 MULTIPLE-CHOICE QUESTION FORMATS

Multiple-choice questions consist of a stem (the question) and four answer choices (response items). Usually one answer is correct and three answer choices (distractors) are incorrect. Another view is that there is one answer choice that is the best response to the question stem. A traditional CPA multiple-choice question appears below.

1. Which of the following is a validity check?

A. The computer ensures that a numerical amount in a record does not exceed some predetermined amount.

B. As the computer corrects errors and data are successfully resubmitted to the system, the causes of the errors are printed out.

C. The computer flags any transmission for which the control field value did not match that of an existing file record.

D. After data are entered, the computer sends certain data back to the terminal for comparison with data originally sent.

 On the CPA exam, expect most of the multiple-choice questions for AUD and the law portion of REG to be conceptual, and expect BEC, FAR, and the tax portion of REG multiple-choice questions to be a mix of conceptual and computational.

Note that some multiple-choice questions contain words like *except*, *not*, *unless*, *least*, etc., as illustrated below.

> According to the FASB's conceptual framework, which of the following attributes should **not** be used to measure inventory?
>
> An auditor may **not** issue a qualified opinion when...

These negative stems ask for the false answer choice, which is accompanied by three true answer choices. Expect a few multiple-choice questions with negative stems on the exam. The AICPA may or may not print these **negative** words in bold type, as illustrated above.

4.3 LESS TRADITIONAL MULTIPLE-CHOICE QUESTION FORMATS

Other types of multiple-choice questions include

1. Questions with two or three answer options
2. Questions with two, three, or four variables in each answer
3. Graphic representations

Occasionally, the AICPA converts two- and three-answer multiple-choice questions into four-answer multiple-choice questions (see question 2 below). When answering questions like these, mark each of the I, II, and IIIs as true or false. Other multiple-choice questions have several variables (or answers) within each answer option and are presented in columns. When answering questions like these, circle the correct answer in each column (see question 3 below).

2. Jewel, CPA, audited Infinite Co.'s prior-year financial statements. These statements are presented with those of the current year for comparative purposes without Jewel's auditor's report, which expressed a qualified opinion. In drafting the current year's auditor's report, the current auditor should

I. Not name Jewel as the predecessor auditor
II. Indicate the type of opinion expressed by Jewel
III. Indicate the reasons for Jewel's qualification

   A.   I only.
   B.   I and II only.
   C.   II and III only.
   D.   I, II, and III.

3. Under the Fair Labor Standards Act, which of the following pay bases may be used to pay covered, nonexempt employees who earn, on average, the minimum hourly wage?

	Hourly	Weekly	Monthly
A.	Yes	Yes	Yes
B.	Yes	Yes	No
C.	Yes	No	Yes
D.	No	Yes	Yes

Yet other questions require graphical interpretation, as illustrated in question 4 below.

4. Using regression analysis, Fairfield Co. graphed the following relationship of its cheapest product line's sales with its customers' income levels:

If there is a strong statistical relationship between the sales and customers' income levels, which of the following numbers best represents the correlation coefficient for this relationship?

   A.   −9.00
   B.   −0.93
   C.   +0.93
   D.   +9.00

4.4 TOOLBAR ICONS AND NAVIGATION

The Prometric presentation of multiple-choice questions does not label answers as A, B, C, and D. To select an answer, click the answer or the radio button (circle) to the left of each answer choice. All of these screenshots were taken from the AICPA website (www.aicpa.org) Sample Test multiple-choice testlet. The CPA exam, the Sample Test, and all of our screenshots are Copyright 2014 by the AICPA with All Rights Reserved. The AICPA requires all candidates to review the Sample Test and Tutorials and be thoroughly familiar with the exam's functionality, format, and directions before sitting for the CPA exam.

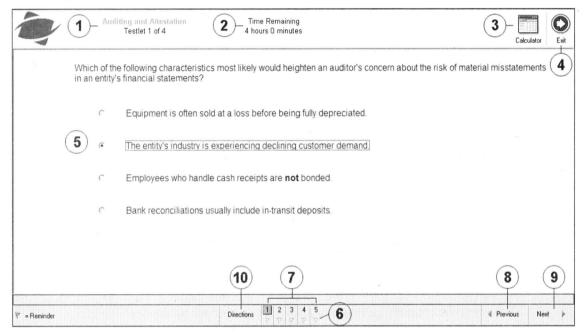

Figure 4-1

1. **Exam Section and Testlet Number:** Multiple-choice will be testlet 1, 2, or 3.

2. **Time Remaining:** Always presented in hours and minutes. Use the Gleim Time Management System explained in Study Unit 7 (pages 59 through 60).

3. **Calculator:** AICPA on-screen calculator. Practice using it in Gleim CPA Test Prep and CPA Gleim Online.

4. **Exit:** Click to end testlet. You will be given three options: Review Testlet, Continue Exam, or Quit Exam.

5. **Answer Choice:** Click to select.

6. **Reminder:** Click to select any question you wish to return to before ending the testlet. Keep these to a minimum on both your practice tests and on your real CPA exam.

7. **Question Status List:** Blue is answered, red flag is set for reminder; click on any question number to go to that question.

8. **Previous:** Move to previous question.

9. **Next:** Move to next question.

10. **Directions:** This screen from Prometric provides insight on the functionality of multiple-choice navigation. Remember that the Gleim Premium CPA Review System has thousands of exam-emulating CPA questions on which you can practice.

4.5 QUESTION-ANSWERING TECHNIQUE

The following suggestions are to assist you in maximizing your score on the multiple-choice testlets that appear in each section of the CPA exam. Remember, knowing how to take the exam and how to answer individual questions is important while you study and review the subject matter tested.

1. **Budget your time.** We make this point with emphasis. Just as you would fill up your gas tank prior to reaching empty, so too would you finish your exam before time expires.

    a. Note that the Time Allocation table in Study Unit 7 budgets about 1.5 minutes for each question and you must save time to return to flagged questions. Before beginning your first testlet of multiple-choice questions, prepare a Gleim Time Management Sheet as recommended in Study Unit 7.

    b. As you work through the individual items, monitor your time. In AUD and FAR, for example, we suggest 45 minutes for each testlet of 30 questions. If you answer five items in 7 minutes, you are fine, but if you spend 10 minutes on five items, you need to speed up.

    NOTE: Remember to allocate your budgeted "extra time" per testlet as needed. Your goal is to answer all of the items and achieve the maximum score possible.

2. **Answer the questions in consecutive order.**

    a. Do **not** agonize over any one item or question. Stay within your time budget.

    b. For any questions you are unsure of, make your best educated guess, flag for review, and return to them later as time allows.

        1) Once you have selected either the Continue or Quit option, you will no longer be able to review/change any answers in the completed testlet.

    c. Never leave a multiple-choice item unanswered. **Make your best educated guess in the time allowed.** Remember that your score is based on the number of correct responses. You will not be penalized for guessing incorrectly.

3. **For each multiple-choice question,**

    a. **Try to ignore the answer choices.** Do not allow the answer choices to affect your reading of the question.

        1) If four answer choices are presented, three of them are incorrect. They are called **distractors** for good reason. Often, distractors are written to appear correct at first glance until further analysis.

        2) In computational items, the distractors are carefully calculated such that they are the result of making common mistakes. Be careful, and double-check your computations if time permits.

    b. **Read the question carefully** to determine the precise requirement.

        1) Focusing on what is required enables you to ignore extraneous information, to focus on the relevant facts, and to proceed directly to determining the correct answer.

            a) Be especially careful to note when the requirement is an **exception**; e.g., "Which of the following is **not** valid acceptance of an offer?"

    c. **Determine the correct answer** before looking at the answer choices.

    d.   **Read the answer choices carefully.**

        1)   Even if the first answer appears to be the correct choice, do **not** skip the remaining answer choices. Questions often ask for the "best" of the choices provided. Thus, each choice requires your consideration.

        2)   Treat each answer choice as a true/false question as you analyze it.

    e.   **Click on the best answer.**

        1)   You have a 25% chance of answering the question correctly by blindly guessing; improve your odds with educated guessing.

        2)   For many multiple-choice questions, two answer choices can be eliminated with minimal effort, thereby increasing your educated guess to a 50-50 proposition.

4.   After you have answered all the items in a testlet, consult the question status list at the bottom of each multiple-choice question screen **before** clicking the Exit button, which permanently ends the testlet.

    a.   Go back to the flagged questions and finalize your answer choices.

    b.   Verify that all questions have been answered.

5.   Remember to stay on schedule. Time control is critical.

4.6 EDUCATED GUESSING

The CPA exam sometimes includes questions that are poorly worded or confusing. Expect the unexpected and move forward. Do not let confusing questions affect your concentration or take up too much time; make your best guess and move on.

If you don't know the answer, make an educated guess. First, rule out answers that you think are incorrect. Second, speculate on what the AICPA is looking for and/or the rationale behind the question. Third, select the best answer or guess between equally appealing answers. However, unless you made an obvious mistake or computational error, try to avoid changing answers. Your first guess is usually the most intuitive.

If you cannot make an educated guess, read the stem and each answer and pick the most intuitive answer. It's just a guess!

4.7 TIME ALLOCATION

Allocate 1.5 minutes to each multiple-choice question no matter which section you are taking. See the time allocations detailed in Table 1 in Study Unit 7, Subunit 10. Note that you have 3-4 extra minutes for each testlet. In order to optimize the time remaining, you need to understand time budgeting based on what you are going to experience at the exam. Table 2 in Study Unit 7, Subunit 10, shows the time remaining at the end of each testlet given your use of our recommended time budget. Our recommended time budgeting results in 15 minutes of extra time for breaks and a safety net. In other words, any time you take for breaks plus the time you spend beyond our recommended times has to come out of the safety net.

4.8 MULTIPLE-CHOICE TIME BUDGETING AND CONTROL TECHNIQUES WITH GLEIM PRACTICE EXAMS

Using the Gleim study system, you will do a **minimum** of two Practice Exams for each study unit to help you answer multiple-choice questions in 1.5 minutes each. Practice makes perfect!

Live by and thrive on 20-question Practice Exams. They are of sufficient length to challenge you but are not too long. Based on decades of experience, we are very confident that you will have no trouble completing 30-question testlets in 45 minutes or 24-question testlets in 35 minutes on the CPA exam after extensive practice with 20-question exams.

Each Practice Exam should be completed in 30 minutes (plus 10 minutes for review) under exam conditions. Practice "flagging" questions you wish to return to, but always select the best answer for each question on your first pass.

It is imperative that you review each question you flagged and/or answered incorrectly after you have completed each exam. Analyze and understand why you answered each question incorrectly. This step is an essential learning activity because you learn more from each question of which you were unsure or answered incorrectly than from questions answered correctly. In other words, you learn from your mistakes as we all do. It is important to learn and understand the subject matter tested **and** how to answer questions when you are unsure of the correct answer.

4.9 LEARNING FROM YOUR MISTAKES

Learning from questions you answer incorrectly is very important. Each question you answer incorrectly is an **opportunity** to avoid missing actual test questions on your CPA exam. Thus, you should carefully study the answer explanations provided until you understand why the original answer you chose is wrong as well as why the correct answer indicated is correct. This learning technique is clearly the difference between passing and failing for many CPA candidates.

Also, you **must** determine why you answered questions incorrectly and learn how to avoid the same error in the future. Reasons for missing questions include

1. Misreading the requirement (stem)
2. Not understanding what is required
3. Making a math error
4. Applying the wrong rule or concept
5. Being distracted by one or more of the answers
6. Incorrectly eliminating answers from consideration
7. Not having any knowledge of the topic tested
8. Using a poor educated guessing strategy

It is also important to verify that you answered correctly for the right reasons (i.e., read the discussion provided for the correct answers. Otherwise, if the material is tested on the CPA exam in a different manner, you may not answer it correctly.

STUDY UNIT FIVE
TASK-BASED SIMULATIONS AND
WRITTEN COMMUNICATIONS

(14 pages of outline)

There is one task-based simulation testlet in the AUD, FAR, and REG sections of the exam; it is testlet 4, and it accounts for 40% of your total score. Per the AICPA, every work tab is worth the same amount of points, including the Research tab. In BEC, the fourth testlet is Written Communications, and it accounts for 15% of your total score.

5.1 TASK-BASED SIMULATIONS -- TOOLBAR ICONS AND OPERATIONS

Task-based simulations are constructive-response questions that require a candidate to complete six or seven work tasks using information given with the question or provided in Information tabs. Work tabs may ask you to enter amounts or formulas into a spreadsheet, choose the correct answer from a list in a pop-up box, or complete accounting or tax forms. You will also have to complete a Research task, which requires you to research the relevant authoritative literature and cite the appropriate guidance as indicated.

The following information and toolbar icons are located at the top of the testlet screen of each task-based simulation. All of these screen shots are taken from the AICPA website (www.aicpa.org) sample test simulation. The CPA exam, the Sample Test, and all of our screenshots are Copyright 2014 by the AICPA with All Rights Reserved. The AICPA requires all candidates to review the Sample Tests and Tutorials before sitting for the CPA exam.

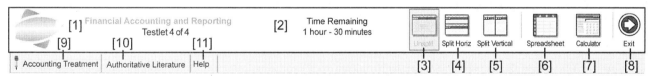

Figure 5-1

1. **Exam Section and Testlet Number:** The testlet number will always be 4 of 4 for the simulations.

2. **Time Remaining:** This information box displays to the examinee how long (s)he has remaining in the entire exam. Consistently check the amount of time remaining in order to stay on schedule.

3. **Unsplit:** This icon, when selected, will unsplit the screen between two tabs.

4. **Split Horiz:** This icon, when selected, will split the screen horizontally between two tabs, enabling you to see, for example, both the simulation question and the help tab at the same time.

5. **Split Vertical:** This icon, when selected, will split the screen vertically between two tabs, enabling you to see, for example, both the simulation question and the help tab at the same time.

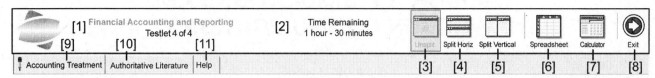

Figure 5-1

6. **Spreadsheet:** The spreadsheet operates like most others and is provided as a tool available for complex calculations. You may enter and execute formulas as well as enter text and numbers.

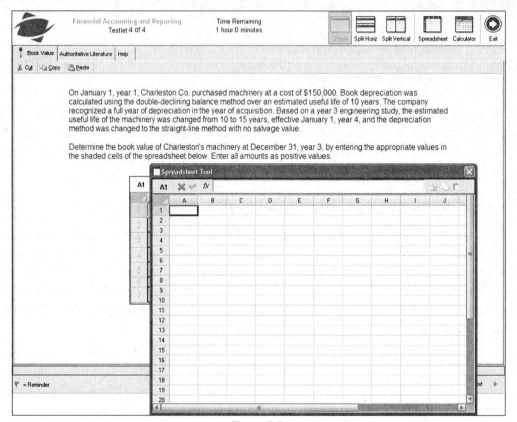

Figure 5-2

7. **Calculator:** The calculator provided is a basic tool available for simple computations. It is similar to calculators used in common software programs.

8. **Exit:** There are two options when you choose this icon from the last testlet:

   - You may choose Review Testlet to return to the beginning of the testlet to review your answers. You will be able to change your answers.

   - You may choose Quit Exam, which means either that you have completed the exam or that you chose not to complete it. Your exam will end and you will not be able to return to any testlet. You will not receive credit for any questions that you have not answered, and you will be required to leave the test center with no re-admittance. If you chose not to complete the exam, there are security measures in place to determine that you are intentionally not completing the exam.

9. **Work Tabs:** A work tab requires the test taker to respond to given information. Each task will have at least one work tab (distinguished by a pencil icon), and each work tab will have specific directions that you must read in order to complete the tab correctly. You must complete all the work tabs in each task to maximize your chance for full credit. There are different varieties of work tabs; the one in the toolbar on the previous page is just an example. You may encounter work tabs that require you to complete forms, fill in spreadsheets, or select an option from multiple choices. See below and on the following pages for an example of each variety of work tab.

   a. **Forms Completion** - This type of work tab will contain a task that requires completion of accounting or tax forms. This task could include the completion of certain sections of tax return forms for personal or corporate taxes, or it could include the completion of other forms of a regulatory nature.

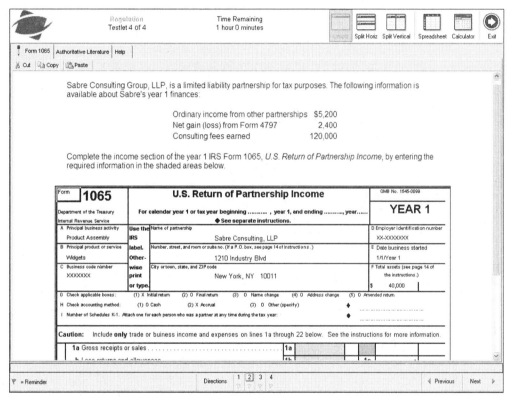

Figure 5-3

b. **Multiple Choice/Multiple Select** - This type of work tab will contain tasks that will be answered through the multiple-choice/multiple selection method. Many of these will be pop-up boxes containing the possible answers. You may need to double-click the cell to produce the pop-up box.

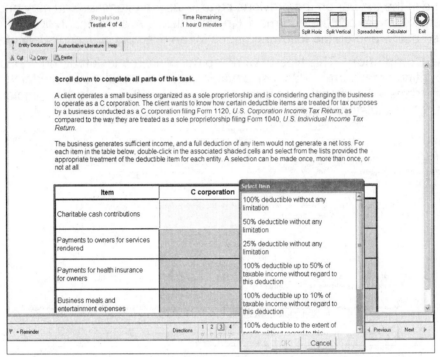

Figure 5-4

c. **Spreadsheet Response** - This work tab will contain tasks that require completion of specific functions within a spreadsheet. This could include the completion of an equity section of a balance sheet, the completion of an indirect cash flow statement, or a calculation of inventory amounts. Accordingly, you may need to enter (1) numbers or monetary amounts (Figure 5-5) or (2) formulas. For the latter, you will have the option to use a Formula Editor, which will supply you with editable copies of various formulas you may need.

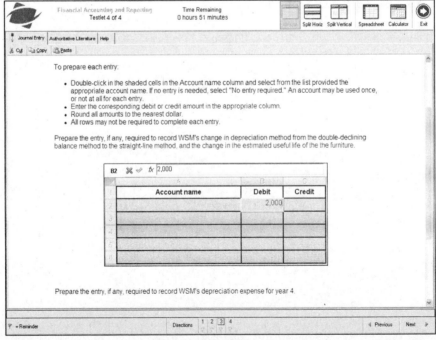

Figure 5-5

d. **Research** - Research tabs require that you search the Authoritative Literature for the appropriate guidance on the issue presented. To answer a Research tab, follow these steps:

1) Read the question and understand what it is asking.

2) Click on the Authoritative Literature tab, and use either the Table of Contents or the Search Engine function to locate the correct guidance.

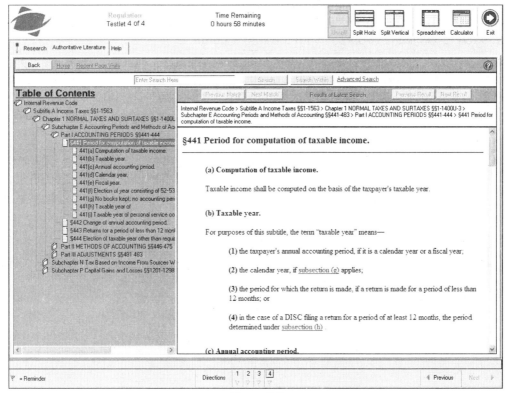

Figure 5-6

3) Once you have found the guidance you need, go back to the Research tab and enter the citation as prompted.

a) The AICPA provides free access to the professional literature used in the simulation questions. CPA candidates can get a free 6-month subscription to a literature package, which includes FASB Accounting Standards Codification™. Only candidates who have received their NTS (Notice to Schedule) will receive free access to this literature. Educators can obtain free access to this literature, and students may access it by paying a small fee.

i) Visit the AICPA's exam website, www.aicpa.org, to access the Professional Literature. You will need the information on your NTS to register for free access.

b) **With this literature and the simulations in the Gleim Premium CPA Review System, CPA candidates can emulate the simulations as they appear on the Prometric exam.**

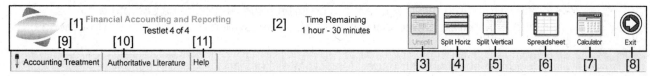

Figure 5-1

10. **Information Tabs:** An information tab gives you information to help with responding to work tabs. Each task will have at least one information tab (the Authoritative Literature, as explained in item a. below). If your task has additional information tabs (see item b. below, for example), go through each to familiarize yourself with the task's content.

    a. **Authoritative Literature** - Every work task in every simulation will have an Authoritative Literature tab to be used for additional research (seen in Figure 5-6). The available content differs based on the section of the exam, but the functions are the same.

    b. **Resources** - Resource tabs contain various resources and tools for use with the current work task. They will vary depending upon the work task. See Figure 5-7 below.

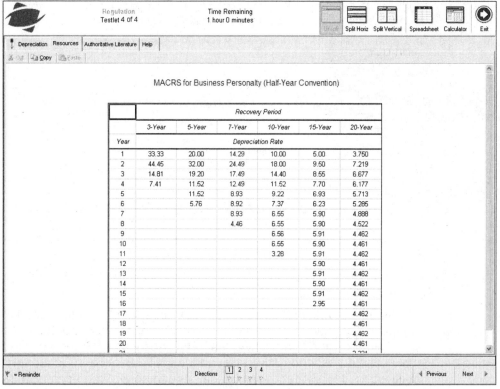

Figure 5-7

11. **Help:** This tab, when selected, provides a quick review of certain functions and tool buttons specific to the type of task you are working in. It will also provide directions and general information but will not include information related specifically to the test content.

Practicing the simulation questions prior to sitting for the CPA exam is vital. You do not want to waste valuable exam time learning how to use the simulations.

5.2 TASK-BASED SIMULATIONS -- QUESTION-ANSWERING TECHNIQUES

Do NOT be intimidated by simulations. Do your best so you outperform one out of two candidates. Practice answering simulation questions in the Gleim Premium CPA Review System. Each study unit has six or seven unique practice simulations, depending on the section.

The following suggestions will assist you in maximizing your score on the simulation testlets on each section of the CPA exam. Remember, knowing how to work through the simulations in an efficient manner is nearly as important as studying/reviewing the subject matter tested on the exam.

1. Budget your time. Within the total time for the simulation testlet, you must allot smaller segments of time to specific tasks. It is vital to track your progress to ensure that you have enough time to complete all of the tasks.

    a. The discussion of a time management system in Subunit 5.3, "Task-Based Simulations -- Time Allocation," contains more information on this subject.

2. Use the first minute or two to read the directions.

    a. Do not spend more than a couple of minutes reading the directions. If you are studying with the Gleim Premium CPA Review System, you have been using an exact emulation of the simulations on the exam.

3. Allocate the next 90 minutes to answer all of the tasks in order from left to right.

    a. Complete each task in no more than 13 minutes.
    b. Attempt to complete each tab before moving on to the next tab. However, if you become frustrated, have difficulty, etc., move on to the next tab.

4. Now you have spent 90 minutes of the 105 minutes available. Spend your remaining 15 minutes wisely to maximize your points earned.

    a. Ask yourself where you will pick up the most points. Move from task to task systematically, reviewing and completing each one.

5.3 TASK-BASED SIMULATIONS -- TIME ALLOCATION

Recall that each of the four testlets in AUD, FAR, and REG are independent. There are no time limits on individual testlets. Thus, you must budget your time so you can complete all four testlets within the total time allowed. We believe you should use the following time-allocation suggestions as a guide. Pages 59 through 60 contain specific time-management instructions.

Since AUD and FAR each have a total testing time of 4 hours, we suggest you allocate 90 minutes for the Task-Based Simulation testlet. REG, however, is only 3 hours in length; therefore, you should allocate only 60 minutes for the simulation testlet.

You must also portion out your time for each task within the simulation testlet. AUD and FAR contain seven tasks each. We suggest you spend no more than 13 minutes on each task. REG contains six tasks, so you should not spend longer than 10 minutes on any one of them. Table 1 in Study Unit 7, Subunit 10, has more information on time allocation.

In order to optimize the time remaining, you need to understand time budgeting based on what you are going to experience at the exam. Table 2 in Study Unit 7, Subunit 10, shows the time remaining at the end of each testlet given your use of our recommended time budget, which results in 15 minutes of extra time for breaks and a safety net. In other words, any time you take for breaks plus the time you spend beyond our recommended times has to come out of the safety net.

Time budgeting is discussed in more detail in Study Unit 7. For now, focus on completing each task you practice in 10-13 minutes.

5.4 WRITTEN COMMUNICATIONS -- TOOLBAR ICONS AND OPERATIONS

In the BEC section of the exam, your last testlet will be the written communication tasks, which test your ability to logically organize and communicate information. This testlet will contain three written communication scenarios (two graded, one pretest) that you must respond to in the form of a memo by typing with a word processor. The following information and toolbar icons are located at the top of the testlet screen and are described below. The AICPA requires all candidates to review the sample tests and tutorial before sitting for the CPA exam.

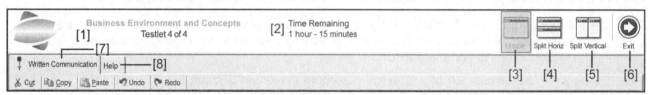

Figure 5-8

1. **Exam Section and Testlet Number:** For BEC, this part of the toolbar will always show Business Environment and Concepts as the Exam Section and Testlet 4 of 4 as the Testlet Number.

2. **Time Remaining:** This information box displays to the examinee how long (s)he has remaining in the entire exam. Consistently check the amount of time remaining in order to stay on schedule for completion.

3. **Unsplit:** This icon, when selected, will unsplit the screen between two tabs.

4. **Split Horiz:** This icon, when selected, will split the screen horizontally between two tabs, enabling you to see, for example, both the written communication scenario and the help tab at the same time.

5. **Split Vertical:** This icon, when selected, will split the screen vertically between two tabs, enabling you to see, for example, both the written communication scenario and the help tab at the same time.

6. **Exit:** There are two options when you choose this icon from the written communication testlet:

    a. You may choose Review Testlet to return to the beginning of the testlet to review your responses. You will be able to change your responses.

    b. You may choose Quit Exam, which means either that you have completed the exam or that you chose not to complete it. Your exam will end and you will not be able to return to any testlet. You will not receive credit for any questions you have not answered, and you will be required to leave the test center with no re-admittance. If you chose to quit your exam before you have completed it, there are security measures in place to determine that you are intentionally not completing the exam.

7. **Written Communication:** This work tab will contain three scenarios, each of which will require you to prepare a written memo or business letter in response. You will be able to cut, copy, paste, undo, and redo by clicking on the appropriate icon. An example of a written communication screen is below.

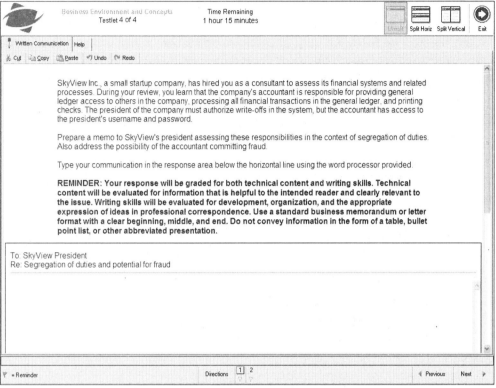

Figure 5-9

8. **Help:** This icon, when selected, provides a quick review of certain functions and tool buttons. It will also provide directions and general information but will not include information related specifically to the test content.

5.5 WRITTEN COMMUNICATIONS -- QUESTION-ANSWERING TECHNIQUES

Do NOT be intimidated by written communications. Do your best so you outperform one out of two candidates. Practice writing responses in your Gleim Premium CPA Review System. Each study unit in the BEC course has at least two unique practice written communications.

Remember, this testlet will have three written communication scenarios, two of which will be graded (one is a pretest). The following suggestions will assist you in maximizing your score on the written communication testlet of the CPA exam. Remember, knowing how to take the exam and how to answer individual questions is nearly as important as studying the subject matter tested on the exam.

1. Budget your time. Within the total time for the Written Communication testlet, you must allot smaller segments of time to each scenario. It is vital to track your progress to ensure that you have enough time to respond to all three scenarios.

    a. The discussion of a time management system in Subunit 5.7, "Written Communications -- Time Allocation," contains more information on this subject.

2. Use the first minute or two to read the directions.

    a. Do not spend more than a couple of minutes reading the directions. If you have been studying with the Gleim Premium CPA Review System, you have been using an exact emulation of the Written Communications on the exam.

3. Allocate the next 60 minutes to respond to all of the scenarios.

    a. Complete each response in no more than 20 minutes.

    b. Do NOT try to guess which is the ungraded pretest scenario. Respond to each scenario as though it counts!

4. Now you have spent 60 minutes of the 75 minutes available. Spend your remaining 15 minutes wisely to maximize your points earned.

    a. Ask yourself where you will pick up the most points. Move from scenario to scenario systematically, reviewing and completing each one.

5.6 WRITTEN COMMUNICATIONS -- ANSWERING AND GRADING

Remember, on the BEC exam, you will respond to three written communication scenarios, two of which will be graded. Your score on those two responses will make up 15% of your total score. The other 85% of your total score will be the sum of your scores on the multiple-choice testlets.

> Your BEC Written Communications may cover topics outside the scope of the BEC CSO (i.e., they may relate to topics from the AUD, FAR, and/or REG CSOs instead). Gleim includes written communication scenarios that cover all topics from all four sections of the exam in the Gleim system to ensure you are prepared. Also, while the graders are mainly evaluating your writing ability and will overlook minor technical mistakes, they will take content into account if your response contains egregious factual errors, off-topic information, or illegal advice. Therefore, you should (1) try to respond to each Written Communication as clearly as possible and (2) ensure that your response is free from off-topic or drastically incorrect information.

In the written communication on the BEC exam, you will be graded on both technical content and writing skills. The AICPA's Sample Test states that the "technical content will be evaluated for information that is helpful to the intended reader and clearly relevant to the issue." It also states that writing skill scores will be based on three criteria from the AICPA: organization (structure, ordering of ideas, linking of ideas to one another), development (presentation of supporting evidence), and expression (use of standard business English). The AICPA advises that all responses "should provide the correct information in writing that is clear, complete, and professional. Only those writing samples that are generally responsive to the topic will be graded. If your response is off-topic, or offers advice that is clearly illegal, you will not receive any credit for the response."

Gleim has expanded the definitions of the AICPA's three writing skills criteria below. Note that the italics denote items taken from the AICPA; everything else is further clarification from Gleim.

Organization -- *the document's structure, ordering of ideas, and linking of one idea to another*

- *Overview/thesis statement*: Inform the reader of the overall purpose of the document; i.e., name the subject about which you are attempting to provide information.
- *Unified paragraphs (topic and supporting sentences)*: Make a statement, then use the remainder of the paragraph to back up that statement.
- *Transitions and connectives*: Words such as "because," "although," "however," and "moreover" allow you to connect related topics or shift the reader's attention to a new idea.

Development -- *the document's supporting evidence/information to clarify thoughts*

- *Details*: Simply asserting a fact, such as that debt on the balance sheet increases risk, is insufficient. The writer must describe the cause-and-effect relationship underlying this fact.
- *Definitions*: Accounting and finance terms, such as solvency and liquidity, may not be understood by the reader. The writer should explain them.
- *Examples*: The description of unfamiliar terms can be enhanced by the use of examples, such as the use of an expert system in the practice of distance medicine.
- *Rephrasing*: Stating an idea twice with different wording can also help the reader understand.

Expression -- *the document's use of conventional standards of business English*

- *Grammar (sentence construction, subject/verb agreement, pronouns, modifiers)*: Adherence to the basic rules of English grammar is essential.
- *Punctuation (final, comma)*: A period must be used to bring a complete sentence to a close. Commas should be used to separate items in lists as well as to separate clauses within a single sentence.
- *Word usage (incorrect, imprecise language)*: Business readers expect writers to avoid ambiguity and to choose the right word for the situation; for example, not to use the word "bond" where "note" is meant.
- *Capitalization*: The first word of a sentence and all proper names must be capitalized. Concepts and measures, such as liquidity and earnings per share, are not normally capitalized.
- *Spelling*: Business readers have an expectation that writers have a grasp of standard spelling conventions.

To help you gauge your proficiency in constructing a response that excels in all of the AICPA's criteria, the Gleim Premium CPA Review System allows you to assign a self-grade to your written communication responses. Self-grading your responses for practice written communication tasks will make you an expert on what the AICPA is looking for, and you will be able to quickly assess your response on the actual exam because you have practiced doing so during your studies.

The self-grading section that appears at the end of each study unit in your book mimics the interactive tools available in the Gleim Premium CPA Review System. You will grade yourself on technical content by noting (1) if your response is on-topic, (2) if you have any significant errors in the information you give, and (3) if you give any illegal advice. You will also grade yourself on a scale of 1 to 5 on each of the AICPA's writing skills criteria (organization, development, and expression). An average response is 3. Use 4 for better than average and 5 for outstanding. Use 2 for less than average and 1 for quite poor.

Below and on the following pages you will find a written communication scenario and examples of responses at writing skill levels 1 and 5. These examples are intended to provide you with tips about how to structure sentences and state your ideas when completing written communications on the BEC portion. All other suggested responses provided by Gleim throughout your book and online courses are writing skill level 5 responses that are on-topic and contain no egregious errors or illegal advice.

| Written Communication | Help |

✂ Cut   📋 Copy   📋 Paste   ↩ Undo   ↪ Redo

The partners of Packitup Partnership are considering the decision to convert to the corporate form of business organization. During your discussions with them, you determine that they have only the vaguest ideas about the relationship between corporate debt and equity.

Prepare a memo to the partners of Packitup Partnership describing the concept of solvency, the two main components of corporate capital, and how capital structure decisions affect the risk profile of a firm.

Type your communication below the line in the response area below.

REMINDER: Your response will be graded for both technical content and writing skills. Technical content will be evaluated for information that is helpful to the intended reader and clearly relevant to the issue. Writing skills will be evaluated for development, organization, and the appropriate expression of ideas in professional correspondence. Use a standard business memorandum or letter format with a clear beginning, middle, and end. Do not convey information in the form of a table, bullet point list, or other abbreviated presentation.

To: Packitup Partnership
Re: Solvency and capital structure

⚐ = Reminder   Directions   [1]   ◀ Previous   Next ▶
                                              ▽

Level 5 Example

To: Packitup Partnership
Re: Solvency and capital structure

Solvency is a firm's ability to pay its noncurrent obligations as they come due and thus remain in business in the long run (this is in contrast to liquidity, which is the ability to remain in business in the short run). The key ingredients of solvency are the firm's capital structure and degree of leverage. A firm's capital structure includes its sources of financing, both long- and short-term. These sources can be in the form of debt (external sources) or equity (internal sources).

Debt is the creditor interest in the firm. The firm is contractually obligated to repay debtholders. The terms of repayment (i.e., timing of interest and principal) are specified in the debt agreement. As long as the return on debt capital exceeds the amount of interest paid, the use of debt financing is advantageous to a firm. The return is often enhanced due to the fact that interest payments on debt are tax-deductible. The tradeoff is that an increased debt load makes a firm riskier (since debt must be paid regardless of whether or not the company is profitable). At some point, either a firm will have to pay a higher interest rate than its return on debt or creditors will simply refuse to lend any more money.

Equity is the ownership interest in the firm. Equity is the permanent capital of an entity, contributed by the firm's owners in the hopes of earning a return. However, a return on equity is uncertain because equity embodies only a residual interest in the firm's assets (residual because it is the claim left over after all debt has been satisfied). Periodic returns to owners of excess earnings are referred to as dividends. The firm may be contractually obligated to pay dividends to preferred stockholders but not to common stockholders.

Capital structure decisions affect the risk profile of a firm. For example, a company with a higher percent of debt capital will be riskier than a firm with a higher percentage of equity capital. Thus, when the relative amount of debt is high, equity investors will demand a higher rate of return on their investments to compensate for the risk brought about by the high degree of financial leverage. Alternatively, a company with a relatively larger proportion of equity capital will be able to borrow at lower rates because debt holders will accept lower interest in exchange for the lower risk indicated by the equity cushion.

The previous page shows an example of a Level 5 response.

Organization. The assignment requires that three concepts be explained: solvency, components of the capital structure, and the effect on the risk profile. This memo does that in a logically structured fashion, with the ideas ordered in a way that makes sense, and with each idea leading to the next.

Development. In this memo, debt and equity are presented as having their own risk and reward characteristics. However, this is not simply asserted as a fact to be taken for granted, but is demonstrated by the explanation of tax-deductibility, dividend payments, etc. Thus, the document's supporting evidence/information clarifies the thoughts presented.

Expression. The conventional standards of business English are observed throughout. Overall, use of the semi-colon is limited, and commas are used appropriately to separate clauses. The last sentence is somewhat lengthy, but it is not a run-on sentence; that is, it only consists of two clauses, one containing an assertion and the other containing the support for that assertion.

Level 1 Example

To: Packitup Partnership
Re: Solvency and capital structure

Debt and equity are the two ways that a corporation can raise capital, and they have to stay solvent that way. They are solvent because debt is part of the capital structure and equity is the other part. Debt is from those outside the firm and equity is from those inside.

However, debt which is bonds have to pay interest but the company can deduct interest on bonds. But this is riskier to the firm because they have to pay the interest no matter what.

Equity though is stock which is the ownership of the firm. But the company has to pay a higher return on stockholders than they do on bondholders because these are dividends that they pay to the stockholders but they are not required to pay dividends which they are required to do on bonds and interest. There is also preferred stock.

So you can have:

- Debt
- Common stock
- Preferred stock

BTW If there is more debt there is more risk and there is more leverage.

The above shows an example of a Level 1 response. It fulfills the two base requirements (it addresses the topic and does not offer advice that is clearly illegal), but beyond this it does not succeed at its goal of clearly communicating information.

Organization. Relevant ideas are scattered throughout the document with no attempt at creating a flow. For instance, after the three forms of capital are recapped in the bullet list, a new idea is introduced. The run-on sentence in the third paragraph destroys any sense of organization the material might have had.

Development. The second paragraph is an example of how pertinent concepts can be mentioned but not developed. Notice that the writer properly presents two concepts central to the discussion: debt, and the associated risk that results from the need to never miss an interest payment. The effectiveness is then immediately diminished by the careless use of connective words: "however" appears once and "but" appears twice in the space of two sentences. Used this way, these words do nothing more than jam the ideas together without actually telling the reader how they relate. Connectors such as "but" and "however" can be useful in establishing a flow or a hierarchy of ideas, but this writer has not done that. Another example of lack of connection is the introduction of the idea of preferred stock at the end of the third paragraph with no attempt to relate it to what has come before.

Expression. The use of standard business English is important to maintaining the proper tone. For example, commas should be used to set off subordinate ideas from the rest of a sentence. In the third paragraph, the sentence that begins, "Equity though is stock..." is a weak sentence made worse by the absence of commas surrounding "though." In the final sentence of the memo, a comma is needed to separate the basic idea, called the premise (if there is more debt), from the result of that idea, called the conclusion (the firm will carry more risk).

Also, the final sentence jams an additional clause on the end ("...and there is more leverage"), connected with nothing more than the word "and." As this demonstrates, a run-on sentence does not have to be long. The last sentence also contains the use of an acronym common to electronic communication (BTW), which are inappropriate for a business memo. Also, the instructions clearly state that bullet points and other list formats should not be used.

5.7 WRITTEN COMMUNICATIONS -- TIME ALLOCATION

Recall that the four testlets in BEC are independent. There are no time limits on individual testlets. Thus, you must budget your time so you can complete all four testlets within the total time allowed. We believe you should use the following time-allocation suggestions as a guide. Pages 59 through 60 contain specific time-management instructions.

Since BEC has a total testing time of 3 hours, we suggest you allocate 60 minutes for the Written Communication testlet. You must also portion out your time for each of the three scenarios within the testlet: Spend no longer than 20 minutes on each response. Table 1 in Study Unit 7, Subunit 10, has more information on time allocation.

In order to optimize the time remaining, you need to understand time budgeting based on what you are going to experience at the exam. Table 2 in Study Unit 7, Subunit 10, shows the time remaining at the end of each testlet given your use of our recommended time budget, which results in 15 minutes of extra time for breaks and a safety net. In other words, any time you take for breaks plus the time you spend beyond our recommended times has to come out of the safety net.

Time budgeting is discussed in more detail in Study Unit 7. For now, focus on completing each question you practice in 20 minutes or less.

STUDY UNIT SIX
PREPARING TO PASS THE CPA EXAM

(7 pages of outline)

Preparing to sit for the CPA exam requires planning and control, i.e., a control system. This study unit suggests study and preparation procedures to maximize your test scores.

6.1 HOW TO BE IN CONTROL

You have to be in control to be successful during exam preparation and execution. Control is a process that we use in all of our activities, implicitly or explicitly. The objective is to improve performance as well as to be confident that the best possible performance is being generated. **What is control?** Control is a process whereby you

1. Develop expectations, standards, budgets, and plans
2. Undertake activity, production, study, and learning
3. Measure the activity, production, output, and knowledge
4. Compare actual activity with expected and budgeted activity
5. Modify the activity, behavior, or study to better achieve the expected or desired outcome
6. Revise expectations and standards in light of actual experience
7. Continue the process or restart the process in the future

The control process is applicable to all of your endeavors, both professional and personal. You should refine your personal control processes specifically toward passing the CPA exam.

Unless you are a natural at something, most endeavors will improve with explicit control. This is particularly true with the CPA examination.

1. Develop an explicit control system over your study process.

2. Practice your question-answering techniques (and develop control) as you prepare solutions to recent CPA exam questions during your study program.

3. Plan to use the Gleim Time Management System at the exam.

Also, notice the similarity between being prepared and being in control. When you are prepared, you know what to expect and what to do! Preparation is the key to success on the CPA exam: knowing what to expect and what to do to **pass the exam**! Control is exactly what *How to Pass the CPA Exam: A System for Success* and the other components of the Gleim Knowledge Transfer System give you.

6.2 DETERMINE ORDER AND TIMING OF EXAM SECTIONS

Which section should you take first? The section that appeals to you for any reason makes the most sense. Which sections are you most conversant with based on recent classes or work experience?

You have 18 months to pass all four sections. Within this time period, there are six 2-month exam windows. Each window includes the first 2 months of the quarter (e.g., January/February, April/May, etc.). Page 49 contains the 2015 calendar. The shaded months are testing windows. One approach is to take one section per exam window, and retake any section you did not pass, plus a new section, in the next window.

Because the Gleim system will prepare you to outperform your peers in each section, we recommend a more aggressive scheduling approach. The NASBA-issued Notices to Schedule are good for 6 months (two exam windows) in most states. Therefore, you can aim to pass all four sections in just 6 months by taking one section at the beginning and another section near the end of two consecutive exam windows. For example, if you plan to test in the April/May and July/August windows, you can schedule one section each at the beginning of April, mid-May, beginning of July, and end of August. This example provides 6 or more weeks between each exam section. You may wish to configure your individual preferences. For example, taking your second section at the end of May gives you 2 additional weeks to prepare but reduces the time available to study for the July window. Review this calendar on the next page to visualize this approach.

The best outcome is to pass each section of the CPA exam the first time you sit for it. Gleim can help you become part of the elite group that successfully achieves this goal!

6.3 APPLY TO TAKE THE EXAM

After studying the overview of the CPA exam in Study Unit 1 and our suggestions on the order and timing of your exam schedule, decide when and where you will take the exam. Check your upcoming schedule thoroughly to make sure you will have plenty of time to study. You may have to gather application information from several state boards before making your decision, and the application process differs based on the state you choose.

Be sure to complete your application correctly. If information is incorrect or missing, the application will be returned and you may not have time to resubmit it before your desired test date. Also, be very careful to specify which sections you are taking.

6.4 STUDY PLAN

Once you have applied for your first section, complete study unit after study unit in sequential order. Remember that you will never be completely prepared AND you may have to go on to the next study unit with a 75% (or less) correct response rate on multiple-choice questions. Stay on schedule and focus on a reasonable and attainable objective: PASSING!

The Gleim CPA Review program consists of 20 study units per exam section, or a total of 80 study units for all four sections of the exam. Allocate time to study Study Units 1 through 7 in this *How to Pass the CPA Exam: A System for Success* booklet.

It is imperative to plan your study schedule well in advance of the CPA exam. Once you have received your NTS, log in to your Gleim Personal Classroom at www.gleim.com to set up your Study Planner. The Gleim Study Planner will help you stay on track, notify you if you fall behind, and provide performance feedback.

2015 CPA CALENDAR

	Sun	Mon	Tues	Wed	Thurs	Fri	Sat
JAN					1	2	3
	4	5	6	7	8	9	10
	11	12	13	14	15	16	17
	18	19	20	21	22	23	24
	25	26	27	28	29	30	31
FEB	1	2	3	4	5	6	7
	8	9	10	11	12	13	14
	15	16	17	18	19	20	21
	22	23	24	25	26	27	28
MAR	1	2	3	4	5	6	7
	8	9	10	11	12	13	14
	15	16	17	18	19	20	21
	22	23	24	25	26	27	28
APR	29	30	31	1	2	3	4
	5	6	7	8	9	10	11
	12	13	14	15	16	17	18
	19	20	21	22	23	24	25
MAY	26	27	28	29	30	1	2
	3	4	5	6	7	8	9
	10	11	12	13	14	15	16
	17	18	19	20	21	22	23
	24	25	26	27	28	29	30
JUN	31	1	2	3	4	5	6
	7	8	9	10	11	12	13
	14	15	16	17	18	19	20
	21	22	23	24	25	26	27
	28	29	30				

	Sun	Mon	Tues	Wed	Thurs	Fri	Sat
JUL				1	2	3	4
	5	6	7	8	9	10	11
	12	13	14	15	16	17	18
	19	20	21	22	23	24	25
AUG	26	27	28	29	30	31	1
	2	3	4	5	6	7	8
	9	10	11	12	13	14	15
	16	17	18	19	20	21	22
	23	24	25	26	27	28	29
SEP	30	31	1	2	3	4	5
	6	7	8	9	10	11	12
	13	14	15	16	17	18	19
	20	21	22	23	24	25	26
OCT	27	28	29	30	1	2	3
	4	5	6	7	8	9	10
	11	12	13	14	15	16	17
	18	19	20	21	22	23	24
	25	26	27	28	29	30	31
NOV	1	2	3	4	5	6	7
	8	9	10	11	12	13	14
	15	16	17	18	19	20	21
	22	23	24	25	26	27	28
DEC	29	30	1	2	3	4	5
	6	7	8	9	10	11	12
	13	14	15	16	17	18	19
	20	21	22	23	24	25	26
	27	28	29	30	31		

NOTE: Shaded months are available for testing. While the non-shaded months are still part of a window, they are closed for testing.

Figure 6-1

6.5 WHEN AND WHERE TO STUDY

You should study when you study best, i.e., whenever you are most productive and able to focus. Unfortunately, other activities compete for your time. CPA preparation should not be your last priority.

Determine what time-consuming activities you can temporarily give up or defer. Set up a regular schedule with goals regarding how much you will complete in one sitting. This will give you a feeling of accomplishment.

Study wherever you can concentrate. Gleim CPA Review is presented in multimedia for your convenience. Home, work, public transportation, hotels, libraries, and restaurants are all possible study areas. Find study times and areas that are quiet, well lit, and free of distractions.

6.6 PRELIMINARY TESTING: GLEIM CPA DIAGNOSTIC QUIZ

The Gleim CPA Diagnostic Quiz provides a representative sample of 40 multiple-choice questions for each exam section. You should use this tool to determine which section of the exam you want to take first and/or how much time you need to devote to studying particular topic areas (i.e., what your strengths and weaknesses are).

When you have completed the quiz, you will be able to access a Review Session, where you can study answer explanations for the correct and incorrect answer choices of the questions you answered. You will also have the option to consult with a Personal Counselor in order to better focus your review on any areas in which you have less confidence.

For smartphone users, there is also a Gleim Diagnostic Quiz App for iPhone, iPod Touch, and Android. Our website (www.gleim.com/QuizCPA) contains more information.

Candidates who have already purchased the Gleim CPA Review System should skip the Diagnostic Quiz and immediately follow the steps below and on the next page, which incorporate study-unit-specific diagnostic testing.

6.7 HOW TO USE THE GLEIM REVIEW SYSTEM

To ensure that you are using your time effectively, we have formulated a three-step process to apply to each study unit that includes all components together.

Step 1: Diagnostic

    a.   Multiple-Choice Quiz #1 (30 minutes, plus 10 minutes for review) – In Gleim Online, complete Multiple-Choice Quiz #1 in 30 minutes. This is a diagnostic quiz, so it is expected that your scores will be lower.

         1)   Immediately following the quiz, review the questions you marked and/or answered incorrectly. This step is essential to identifying your weak areas. "Learning from Your Mistakes" on page 32 has tips on how to learn from your mistakes.

Step 2: Comprehension

    a.   Audiovisual Presentation (30 minutes) – This Gleim Online presentation provides an overview of the study unit. (Use the Gleim CPA Audio Review instead if you're on the go!)

    b.   Gleim Instruct – CPA Video Series (30-90 minutes) – These videos are for customers who prefer live instruction to the slide-show style of the Audiovisual Presentations. Gleim Instruct videos include lectures featuring professors from accredited universities, multiple-choice questions, and detailed examples.

    c.   True/False Quiz (45 minutes) – Complete the True/False quiz in Gleim Online and receive immediate feedback.

    d.   Knowledge Transfer Outline (60-90 minutes) – Study the Knowledge Transfer Outline, particularly the troublesome areas identified from your Multiple-Choice Quiz #1 in Step 1. The Knowledge Transfer Outlines can be studied either online or in the books.

    e.   Multiple-Choice Quiz #2 (30 minutes, plus 10 minutes for review) – Complete Multiple-Choice Quiz #2 in Gleim Online.

        1)   Immediately following the quiz, review the questions you marked and/or answered incorrectly. This step is an essential learning activity. "Learning from Your Mistakes" on page 32 has tips on how to learn from your mistakes.

Step 3: Application

    a.   Task-Based Simulations (90 minutes, including 10 minutes for review) – Complete and review the simulation section in Gleim Online.

        1)   For BEC, you should spend 60 minutes (including 10 minutes for review) to complete and review the written communication section in Gleim Online.

    b.   CPA Test Prep (60 minutes, plus 20 minutes for review) – Complete two 20-question quizzes in CPA Test Prep using the Practice Exam feature. Spend 30 minutes taking each quiz and then spend about 10 minutes reviewing each quiz as needed.

Additional Assistance

1.   Gleim Simulation Wizard – For additional practice, complete task-based simulations (for AUD, FAR, and REG) or written communication tasks (for BEC) as needed.

2.   Core Concepts – These consolidated documents provide an overview of the key points of each subunit that serve as a foundation for learning.

Final Review

1.   CPA Exam Rehearsal (4 hours/240 minutes for AUD and FAR or 3 hours/180 minutes for BEC and REG) – Take the Exam Rehearsal at the beginning of your final review stage. It contains the same amount of multiple-choice questions and task-based simulations (for AUD, FAR, and REG) or written communications (for BEC) as the CPA exam. This will help you identify where you should focus during the remainder of your final review.

2.   CPA Test Prep (10-20 hours) – Use Test Prep to focus on your weak areas identified from your Exam Rehearsal. Also, be sure to do a cumulative review to refresh yourself with topics you learned at the beginning of your studies. View your performance chart to make sure you are scoring 75% or higher.

The times mentioned above and on the previous page are recommendations based on prior candidate feedback and how long you have to answer questions on the actual exam. Each candidate's time spent in any area will vary depending on proficiency and familiarity with the subject matter.

6.8 GLEIM PREMIUM CPA REVIEW SYSTEM

The Gleim Premium CPA Review System contains everything you need to pass the CPA exam on your first try. Our Premium CPA Review System is available as a set and is also offered for each individual section.

Each Gleim Premium CPA Review System includes Access Until You Pass, the Gleim Instruct video lecture series, books, online course, the largest CPA test bank available, and assistance from our accounting experts. The course is split into the following instructional components:

1. Gleim Online – The majority of your coursework will be completed in this component; consider it your home base for studying. Gleim Online includes your interactive study planner, exam-emulating quizzes, the Gleim digital book containing comprehensive outlines and examples, the Gleim Instruct video lecture series, hundreds of Task-Based Simulations/Written Communications, and Audiovisual Presentations. You will also have access to your own mentor, a Personal Counselor, who will offer advice and assistance while you are studying for the exam.

2. Gleim Simulation Wizard, Gleim CPA Test Prep, Gleim Audio Reviews, Gleim Exam Rehearsal – Want even more practice and review? The Gleim Simulation Wizard and CPA Test Prep are the largest banks of Task-Based Simulations/Written Communications and multiple-choice questions available on the market. Both the Gleim Simulation Wizard and CPA Test Prep emulate the Prometric testing environment and provide detailed answer explanations. On the go? Use the Gleim Audio Review component of your Review System, which encourages auditory learning and includes lectures of the most important concepts from the Gleim books. Finally, during your comprehensive final review, take the full-length Gleim Exam Rehearsal, which will help to identify your weak areas.

All components of the Gleim Premium CPA Review System are available anytime and wherever you have access to the Internet. Get access to the first study unit of the review system absolutely free by visiting www.gleim.com/DemosCPA.

6.9 IF YOU HAVE QUESTIONS ABOUT GLEIM MATERIALS

Gleim has an efficient and effective way for candidates who have purchase the Premium CPA Review System to submit an inquiry and receive a response regarding Gleim materials directly through their course. This system also allows you to view your Q&A session in your Gleim Personal Classroom.

Questions regarding the **information in this booklet (study suggestions, studying plans, exam specifics)** should be emailed to personalcounselor@gleim.com.

Questions concerning **orders, prices, shipments, or payments** should be sent via email to customerservice@gleim.com and will be promptly handled by our competent and courteous customer service staff.

For **technical support**, you may use our automated technical support service at www.gleim.com/support, email us at support@gleim.com, or call us at (888) 874-5346.

6.10 USING CANDIDATE PERFORMANCE REPORTS

Historically, each section has had a 40% to 50% pass rate (for first-time and repeat candidates combined). In fact, 30-35% of all candidates sitting pass no sections at all! Thus, the majority of CPA candidates learn that they failed one or more sections. Use the following steps to prepare for successful completion of the CPA exam:

1. **First**, you should analyze your score by AICPA Content Specification Outline (CSO) area by using the "Candidate Performance Report" that may accompany your exam scores. The purpose of the diagnostic performance report is to help candidates identify the relative strengths and weaknesses of their examination performance as they prepare to retake examination sections. Below is a sample of the report that the AICPA designed for the CBT-e exam. Your report will include directions on how to interpret the weaker, comparable, and stronger ratings you received.

Your Performance Compared to Passing Candidates*
by Content Area

Content Area (% of multiple choice questions)	Weaker	Comparable	Stronger
Framework and Standards (17-23%)	Weaker		
Financial Statement Accounts (27-33%)	Weaker		
Specific Transactions/Events (27-33%)			Stronger
Governmental (8-12%)	Weaker		
Not-for-Profit (8-12%)	Weaker		

by Item Type

	Weaker	Comparable	Stronger
Multiple Choice (60%)	Weaker		
Simulations (40%)	Weaker		

*The comparable column is based on those candidates who scored between 75-80 on the examination section as a whole. For more information regarding how this comparison was calculated or for more information on how the examination is scored, please see the CPA Examination web site at www.aicpa.org/cpa-exam.

Figure 6-2

2. **Second**, review your preparation program from the previous CPA exam. What were its strengths and weaknesses? How can it be improved? Most important is your recognition that what you did previously to prepare for the exam and/or to take the exam DID NOT WORK. Accordingly, you need to make adjustments and rededicate your effort to complete the next exam successfully. Please restudy (don't just reread) this study unit and make sure you have the current Gleim Premium CPA Review System.

3. **Third**, prepare a written plan and schedule to prepare for and take the next CPA exam. Remember that, while the CPA exam generally has a pass rate of less than 50% per exam section, virtually all serious candidates eventually pass. You can and will PASS, especially if you make use of the Gleim Premium CPA Review System. Please restudy (don't just reread) this *System for Success* booklet prior to the next CPA exam. GOOD LUCK!

STUDY UNIT SEVEN
HOW TO TAKE THE CPA EXAM

(6 pages of outline)

The purpose of this study unit is to focus on what to expect on test day and how to react. It includes a general explanation of examination site instructions, rules, and procedures. You have to be prepared as to what to expect so you are not distracted from your mission of **passing the exam**!

7.1 HAVE A POSITIVE MENTAL ATTITUDE

You are in control with the Gleim CPA Review System, which is based upon a systematic, thorough review of all material tested on the CPA exam. It is not hit or miss. The Gleim method does not involve guessing about what will appear on the next CPA exam. **You will be prepared for any and all questions.** If a question appears difficult to you, it will be **more** difficult for other candidates.

7.2 STUDY YOUR EXAM SITE LOCATION/PROMETRIC TEST DRIVE

Prometric exam sites vary in how they are operated. Talk to someone who took an exam at the site you plan to use. Ask him or her for information about the site and for any suggestions (s)he might have.

Additionally, make sure you know where the exam site is and how to get there before test day. Some Prometric centers are in hard-to-find locations. Note that many are part of Sylvan Learning Centers.

A few days prior to taking your exam, call your Prometric testing center and confirm your appointment; leave as little as possible to chance. Review Subunits 7.4-7.6 so you are aware of all Prometric rules and regulations.

One way to become familiar with your chosen test site is to do a Prometric Test Drive (register for $30 at www.prometric.com/TestDrive) sometime before your first section. A Test Drive is a 30-minute, real-world, end-to-end practice run at Prometric. You will not receive real CPA questions, but you will be able to experience locating your test site, checking in, and running through a generic sample test.

NOTE: The Test Drive should **not** be used as a replacement for the AICPA's Sample Test or the Gleim Exam Rehearsal.

7.3 THE DAY OF YOUR CPA EXAM

On the day of your exam, plan on getting to the testing site about 30-60 minutes ahead of your appointment time. Leave all study materials in your car or at home. If you must, you can bring snacks, drinks, etc., to the testing site, but you must leave these items in a locker or a designated area. Prometric asks that you arrive 30 minutes early, but they may ask you to wait up to 30 minutes to start your test.

Be sure to wear comfortable clothes. Sweats, shorts, and jeans are very appropriate. Wear layers according to your usual body temperature because you will not be allowed to remove any outerwear once you are in the testing room. Generally, wear what you wear when you are most comfortable studying. Remember that coats, umbrellas, books, and attaché cases cannot be accommodated at the exam site. Thus, you should not take something that you do not want to lose.

7.4 PROMETRIC TEST CENTER RULES

The staff at each test center has been trained in the procedures for the Uniform CPA Examination. They will guide you through the steps developed by the Boards of Accountancy, NASBA, and AICPA. The following is a paraphrased version of the information given in the Candidate Bulletin:

1. You must arrive at the test center at least 30 minutes before your scheduled appointment. If you arrive after your scheduled appointment time, you may forfeit your appointment and not be eligible to have your examination fees refunded. When you arrive, turn off all cell phones, audio alarms on watches, etc.

2. Your examination should begin within 30 minutes of the scheduled start time. If circumstances arise that delay your session more than 30 minutes, you will be given the choice of continuing to wait or rescheduling your appointment.

3. You must place any personal belongings, such as a purse or cell phone, in the storage lockers provided by the test center. You will be given the key to your locker, which must be returned to the test center staff when you leave. The lockers are very small and are not intended to hold large items. Do not bring anything to the test center unless it is absolutely necessary. You may bring soft, foam earplugs with no strings attached for use during your test.

4. You are required to present two forms of identification and your NTS. Your ID will be scanned/swiped in the combined magnetic strip and 2D barcode reader. Then, a scanner will be used to capture an electronic image of your ID and compare printed and encoded data using optical character recognition. You must keep your identification with you at all times. If you leave the testing room for any reason, you will be required to show your identification to be readmitted.

 A number of candidates are denied exam access due to not having their NTS or proper ID. Read the Candidate Bulletin carefully.

5. You will have a digital photograph of your face (i.e., head shot) as well as a digital fingerprint taken. You will also have your fingerprint taken upon re-entry of the test room if you leave for a break.

6. You will be required to turn your pockets out and be scanned with a hand-held metal detector wand.

7. You will be escorted to a workstation by test center staff. You must remain in your seat during the examination, except when authorized to get up and leave the testing room by test center staff. Two noteboards and a marker will be provided to you. You are required to return these to the test center staff when your examination is complete. If you need additional writing space, you may turn in the original noteboards to get a new supply. You must not bring any other paper or pencils to the work station in the testing room. [The only exception to this rule is your Notice To Schedule (NTS). You must bring the NTS to the workstation.]

8. First, you will enter your Launch Code (from your NTS). Then proceed through the introductory screens without delay. There is a 10-minute time limit for these screens; if you exceed 10 minutes, the test session will be terminated. You will not be able to restart the exam, you will forfeit your fees, and you will receive a score of 0. Raise your hand to notify the test center staff if you experience a problem with your computer, an error message appears on the computer screen (do not clear the message), you need additional noteboards, you choose to take a break between testlets (testing time will not be suspended), or you need the test center staff for any other reason.

9. When you finish the examination, quietly leave the testing room, turn in your noteboards, and sign the test center log book. The test center staff will dismiss you after completing all necessary procedures. Keep the Confirmation of Attendance form you receive.

7.5 PROMETRIC TEST CENTER REGULATIONS

According to the Candidate Bulletin, "A standardized environment is necessary to ensure the examination you take is essentially equivalent to the examination all other candidates take. For this reason, all candidates must follow the same regulations." Be sure to review the Prometric regulations before your test day so you do not unknowingly jeopardize your exam.

7.6 CPA CANDIDATE MISCONDUCT AND CHEATING

Author comment: The CPA designation is very special to the accounting profession and deserves your support. If you observe any potential problems, notify your State Board or Dr. Gleim.

The following paragraph is taken verbatim from NASBA's *Uniform CPA Examination: Candidate Bulletin*:

"The Boards of Accountancy, NASBA, and the AICPA take candidate misconduct (including cheating on the Uniform CPA Examination) very seriously. If a board of accountancy determines that a candidate is culpable of misconduct or has cheated, the candidate will be subject to a variety of penalties including, but not limited to, invalidation of grades, disqualification from subsequent examination administrations, and civil and criminal penalties . . . . In cases where candidate misconduct or cheating is discovered after a candidate has obtained a CPA license or certificate, a board of accountancy may rescind the license or certificate."

Be sure to read your Candidate Bulletin so you know the guidelines regarding misconduct and items that are prohibited from the exam site. Also, you may use Study Unit 3, Subunit 2, to refresh yourself on the AICPA's Confidentiality Statement, as it plays a significant role in candidate conduct.

7.7   CHECKING IN AT THE EXAM SITE

Your Notice To Schedule (NTS) from NASBA and your personal identification are crucial. Your NTS contains your exam section ID number, which you use when you log in to your Prometric computer. You will not be allowed to sit for the CPA exam if you do not have your NTS with you at the testing site. Be sure that you completely understand the personal ID rules from NASBA's *Uniform CPA Examination: Candidate Bulletin* so that you do not have trouble on test day.

In addition to presenting your two forms of ID and being photographed, candidates are now asked to place their finger(s) on a scanner so that a digital image of the fingerprint(s) can be taken. Digital fingerprint images will be encrypted and stored electronically together with candidate identification information. On subsequent visits to Prometric test centers—even years later—fingerprint records will be available at check-in for comparison to confirm the identities of candidates. Fingerprint images will also be used to detect any attempt to impersonate CPA candidates. Fingerprinting will be required every time candidates report to test centers. In addition, candidates returning to test rooms after breaks will be asked to have their fingerprints taken again for comparison with the fingerprints captured at the beginning of the session.

7.8   BEGINNING YOUR EXAM

After you check in with your NTS and ID and have been photographed and fingerprinted, you will be escorted to a computer station. Your NTS will contain a "Launch Code" that you will enter on your computer during your log-in process.

Prometric will provide you with an opportunity to view an abbreviated exam introduction. Work through it so you do not miss anything, but do not go over the allotted 10 minutes; at that time, the exam will be terminated and you will not have the option to restart your exam. As you begin the exam, you will do fine because you have experienced the Gleim Prometric exam-emulating screens.

As soon as your exam starts, write up a Gleim Time Management Sheet to help you be in control of your time (discussed on page 60).

7.9   COMPUTER PROBLEMS AT THE EXAM SITE

There is about 1 chance in 100 that you will encounter a computer problem at the exam site. The most common problem requires staff to reboot your computer. At most, you will lose a minute of testing time according to Prometric. If you have a computer problem, stop and tell/show the exam proctor. Do NOT erase any messages on the screen. Do NOT attempt to circumvent or fix the system. It is a Prometric problem. Note the time it occurred and when it is rectified for your appropriate use in the future.

According to NASBA, you should report all computer problems that you believe were not adequately handled by Prometric by emailing candidatecare@nasba.org. Please also let Gleim know about any issues by emailing cpa@gleim.com.

7.10 THE GLEIM TIME MANAGEMENT SYSTEM

A major issue on the CPA exam is time management. The only help you receive is hours and minutes remaining in your test with no guidance for breaks or time allocation to individual testlets.

Let's discuss the Gleim Time Management System. You must budget your time so you can complete four testlets within the 3-4 hours allowed. Recall that you cannot begin a new testlet until you have closed a current testlet and that, once you have closed a testlet, you can no longer go back to it. The key to success is to become proficient in answering multiple-choice questions in less than 1.5 minutes per question. Each BEC and REG multiple-choice testlet contains 24 questions. Each AUD and FAR multiple-choice testlet contains 30 questions.

1. Here are our suggestions for time allocation for each section:

Time Allocation to Multiple-Choice (MC) and Simulation (TBS)/Written Communication (WC) Testlets

Testlet	Format	BEC	REG	AUD	FAR
1	**MC**	**35**	**35**	**45**	**45**
2	**MC**	**35**	**35**	**45**	**45**
3	**MC**	**35**	**35**	**45**	**45**
4	TBS/WC	60	60	90	90
		165	165	225	225
Extra Time*		15*	15*	15*	15*
Total Time Allowed		180	180	240	240

Table 1

*Time remaining based on recommended time budget. The candidate should develop question-answering techniques that will allow the "extra time" to be used for reviewing flagged questions or taking second looks at difficult questions.

2. Since the computer screen shows hours:minutes remaining, you need to focus on hours:minutes, NOT the time on your watch. Throughout your practice on exam questions, always think hours:minutes. Thus, on a perfect exam using the times above, you would start each testlet with the following hours:minutes displayed on-screen:

Completion Times and Time Remaining

	BEC/REG	AUD/FAR
Start	3 hours 0 mins	4 hours 0 mins
After Testlet 1	2 hours 25 mins	3 hours 15 mins
After Testlet 2	1 hour 50 mins	2 hours 30 mins
After Testlet 3	1 hour 15 mins	1 hour 45 mins
After Testlet 4	0 hours 15 mins	0 hour 15 mins

Table 2

3. Next, develop shorthand for hours:minutes. For example, signify 3 hours, 0 minutes as 03:00; 1 hour, 50 minutes as 01:50. The start times for each testlet will be

BEC/REG	AUD/FAR
03:00	04:00
02:25	03:15
01:50	02:30
01:15	01:45

4. Use one side of one noteboard (provided at Prometric) for your Gleim Time Management System at the exam (see our examples below). Thus, as soon as the exam starts, write Testlet 1, 2, 3, and 4 in the left column followed by 03:00, 02:25, 01:50, and 01:15 next to 1, 2, 3, and 4 for BEC and REG. Write 04:00, 03:15, 02:30, and 01:45 next to 1, 2, 3, and 4 for AUD and FAR As you complete each testlet, note when you finish and then start the next testlet.

BEC/REG

Testlet	Start	Finish	Notes
1	03:00		
2	02:25		
3	01:50		
4	01:15		

Figure 7-1

AUD/FAR

Testlet	Start	Finish	Notes
1	04:00		
2	03:15		
3	02:30		
4	01:45		

Figure 7-2

5. Note that Business and Regulation are tight on time. They are only 3 hours in length, whereas AUD and FAR are 4 hours. To partially make up for this difference, BEC and REG only have 24 questions rather than 30 in each of the three multiple-choice testlets.

7.11 GENERAL TIME MANAGEMENT ADVICE

A final note about time management: We have offered suggested time budgets for each testlet of each exam section. These time budgets are **suggestions**. You must establish your multiple-choice and simulation question-answering techniques to develop your personal time budgets.

Practice makes perfect. It is certainly reasonable for you to develop a multiple-choice question-answering technique that results in a per-question rate of 1 minute or 1.25 minutes. This results in even greater amounts of "extra time" to accommodate your general review and review of flagged questions. Alternatively, you can convert your proficient 1-minute-per-question rate to 1.5 minutes per question and **still** have time to spare. Having 30 seconds of additional time per question for one who is accustomed to needing only 1 minute is a great advantage, promotes a positive attitude, and may well generate the exam success you seek.

Any "extra time" you build into your overall budget should be used wisely. The best-case scenario is to allocate the time equally among the testlets to accommodate your review of flagged questions. Ultimately, you want to make full use of all time available versus leaving Prometric early with all of your "extra time" unused.